FUND YOUR FLIP

HOW TO FUND YOUR FIX AND FLIP WITHOUT USING YOUR OWN MONEY

KEVIN AMOLSCH

TABLE OF CONTENTS

Introduction

The year was 2006, and I was a young, motivated mortgage lender. I was doing whatever it took to get deals done, but I had no control over the money, and despite record flexibility with loan approvals, I was denying real estate investors who had solid projects and clear repayment paths. I felt like I was banging my head against the wall. There had to be a better way!

Susan was my mentor and took me under her wing when I started originating loans with her. She had a very small, single-person lending company with a focus on real estate investors. I had borrowed money from her many times in the past, so it was an obvious choice to ask her if I could work with her. She had access to some private money through a wealthy friend of hers and would loan that money to investors who were fixing and flipping houses in Denver. She also knew another gentleman, Jon, who had $100,000 in cash and was asking her to loan it out for him.

Although she never let me lend out her rich friends' money, she did give me Jon's phone number. Jon became my first private-money investor, and I quickly loaned his money to a fix-and-flipper for a small house. The price for the money was four points in origination fees and 15 percent interest. A point is one percent of the loan amount in a fee. I did as Susan had taught me and kept two points for her company and gave the other two points to Jon. Susan gave me 60 percent of the fees as my commission. My cut: $1,200.

It was this deal that gave me the confidence to turn this into a business. Since then, I have helped thousands of real estate investors fund their deals. I have also helped thousands of passive investors find stability with their investing with some great returns—all backed by the asset I understand and love: real estate.

In this book you will learn what nonbank financing and hard money are and how to use them to make yourself rich as a real estate investor. We will discuss how to use hard money to fund your real estate deals for maximum profit. I will include strategies and tips and case studies with analyses of real deals. The second book in this series is for the passive investor. It is that book that teaches you how to earn high yields with little risk and virtually no effort.

I have woven in stories about my personal experiences in hopes that my experience will help you become a better real estate investor. If you are a real estate investor, strap in. You are about to go on a ride down Success Lane, where it is not always smooth, but as long as you don't exit, success is the only destination. I hope you enjoy learning about the fascinating topic of real estate financing without the banks!

Chapter 1

Hard Money: What It Is and Why Investors Use It

When you google "hard money," you will mostly get real estate loan companies, but there is no *Merriam-Webster* definition. Some sites, including Investopedia, argue that hard money is money that is physically hard, like gold or silver, and not a paper or electronic currency. Some consider a hard-money loan as a loan is a loan of last resort. This is untrue, as I will prove.

The term "hard money" is used in real estate to mean loans that are primarily asset based, meaning the real estate is more heavily weighted in a loan decision than the borrower. Back before the crash of 2008, many hard-money lenders were asset-only qualifying. This means that if you had enough equity in the home or had a large enough down payment, you were approved. The joke goes that the lender would ask you to hold a mirror in front of your face, and if it fogged up, you were approved. If you were alive and breathing, you could get the loan. I know hard money was used in many ways, but one that stuck with me was foreclosure bailout. Think about the typical American family. Two parents, two-and-a-half kids, and a dog. In many families, both parents work to support the household. If they have lived in their home for a fair amount of time, it was likely they had substantial equity. If one of the parents lost their income, they would not be able to support all their obligations. Americans live with razor-thin reserves. This poor family started to fall behind on credit cards and then the car loan, and finally…they missed a payment on the house. What happened next?

Before the crash and all the government support, there were three options for this family. They could pay the house off in full, they could bring the entire amount of missed payments current and keep the home, or they could do nothing and lose the house to foreclosure. To pay off the loan, they would need to sell the house or refinance the loan, but their credit would be a wreck. In this example, assuming there is enough equity, a hard-money lender may consider loaning them the money to pay off the mortgage, bailing them out and saving their home. The family would make payments on the new hard-money loan while they repaired their credit, and then a year or two later, refinance the hard-money loan back into a conventional loan. Boom! House saved.

You would not see this today. First, there are too many options for homeowners like payment plans and forbearance agreements, but there are also new regulations stopping hard-money lenders from helping consumers with their primary homes.

THE LOAN BUCKETS

Every loan that is originated for any purpose—which includes car loans, student loans, credit cards, and payday loans—falls into one of two buckets. The first bucket is the consumer bucket. This bucket consists of any loan that is meant to benefit a consumer, such as home mortgages, cars, and credit cards. The other bucket is your commercial or business use bucket, which includes of SBA loans, business start-up loans, or land-development loans. A loan falls into one of these buckets based on the borrower's intent for the money.

If the intent is to use the money to make money, it is a business-purpose loan. If the intent is to personally benefit, like by buying a car, it is a consumer loan. The government has highly regulated consumer lending since the credit crash of 2008. That is when you saw all sorts of regulations, including the SAFE Act (which required mortgage licensing for consumer real estate loans), RESPA, TILA, TRID, and many others. There are also strict foreclosure laws, usury, and disclosure requirements when it comes to consumer loans. For example, you cannot put a term with a balloon on a consumer loan. A balloon means that the entire loan needs to be repaid by a certain date. This is an extremely common practice with hard money. For these reasons, very few hard-money lenders will loan against one's primary home.

THE TRUTH

The truth about hard money in real estate is that it is a nonbank or nonconventional loan usually from a savvy individual or small company. Hard money is mostly known for its flexibility and high costs.

Hard-money companies are frequently funded by the owners and individual investors, and the decisions are made by a person or small group you can communicate with. This is very different from a bank or conventional lender, where the decisions are made behind the curtain with a phantom underwriter or loan committee. Hard-money decisions are made based on what I like to call common sense. Common-sense underwriting provides the flexibility that makes these loans so attractive to real estate investors. If the lender can understand the loan and can see how the loan will be paid back, they will often approve it, regardless of borrower strength. It is about painting the picture of your vision with a clear exit strategy. This does not necessarily mean that borrower financial strength is not considered. Because hard-money lenders can make their own funding decisions, there is no standardization. Each lender will have its own guidelines and its own flexibility to go outside those guidelines. For example, I know some hard-money lenders that won't pull credit or document any income or assets and others that want to see an entire loan package, including tax returns and bank statements. Some require appraisals and down payments, and some do not. This is why it is important for a real estate investor to shop around before deciding on a hard-money lender, and it is OK to have multiple lenders you can rely on.

REHAB LENDERS

Most residential hard-money lenders are what I would call rehab lenders. This simply means they loan on projects that need to be rehabbed or will have some type of value add. Think fix-and-flip. Most hard-money lenders loan based on the property's "after repaired value," or ARV. Because the loan is based on what a property is going to be worth, not what it is worth today, the lender will want to see that the investor is adding value. Let me paint this picture.

We get calls in our office several times a month from investors with the deal of a lifetime. Yes, the best deals you will see in your entire life every few weeks. One example is the investor who calls with an opportunity to buy a house that is near completion. Maybe the house just needs some carpet, and it is ready for final inspection and the certificate of occupancy (CO). The investor will get the CO when the work has been completed and inspected by the city. After the carpet is installed and the investor has the CO, they think the house will sell for $450,000. They can buy the house for, let's say, $350,000. Oh, did I mention that they found the deal in the multiple listing service (MLS)? Does anyone see a problem with this scenario?

OK, so you are telling me you are adding $100,000 in value with some carpet? I already know the house sold at or close to full value because it had ultimate exposure with the MLS. As a lender, I have to believe a house sells at value when listed, because thousands of buyers had access to it. Now I can be wrong, of course, but I find it hard to believe that carpet adds $100,000 in value. That might be a deal I pass on. As a rehab lender, I can tell you that rehab lenders want to see rehab. They want the worst of the worst, so it is easy to justify the large swing in value that is needed for a fix-and-flipper to make money. And by the way, an appraiser will likely want to see the same thing. If you can find houses that are falling over, can have functional improvements, can be increased in size, were occupied by hoarders, or need a complete remodel, those are great candidates for hard-money lenders.

COST

Hard-money loan pricing varies widely. I have heard as little as one point and eight percent interest and as much as six points and 18 percent interest. Most lenders fall somewhere around two to three points and 12 percent interest. Obviously, rates can vary based on market conditions, but hard-money rates are far more stable than bank or conventional loans. So if you borrow $100,000 and there is one point tied to the loan, you will pay the lender a fee of $1,000. Two points would cost you $2,000. The way interest and fees are charged also varies. Some lenders are OK collecting some or all of their fees when you pay off the loan, while most hard-money lenders want to collect their fees up front. Some allow you to roll it into the loan, and some require you pay fees out of pocket. Interest is no different with its flexibility. All the lenders I know charge interest based on an annual rate, but some collect interest up front, some collect the interest when the loan pays off, and some want payments every month. Some lenders have minimum interest charges, while most do not. Minimum interest is one hidden fee to watch out for.

HIDDEN FEES

Hard-money lenders charge multiple fees, and some lenders are more transparent than others. Here are some of the harder-to-see fees that you should keep an eye out for.

Prepayment Penalties

Although rare, in most states there is nothing stopping a hard-money lender from charging penalties for paying off a loan early. This will not show up on your settlement statement or closing disclosure, so it can be difficult to find. The hard-money lender should disclose if there is an early payoff penalty in their term sheet or disclosure packets, so be sure to read those.

Draw and Inspection Fees

Most rehab lenders will want to visit the project to ensure repairs or construction is occurring. If there is a construction holdback, you should expect the lender to do an inspection each time you request a draw. A construction holdback is when the lender holds on to the money for the construction and releases it to you or your contractor based on a schedule that you agree to. These fees are never discussed when speaking to a lender and will only come up in the disclosures or the settlement statement. These fees usually vary from $100 per inspection to $1,000 per inspection. If the lender does their own inspections, it should be cheaper, but if they outsource this—to a title company, for example—it will be more expensive. Assuming the lender does not outsource this task, this is one fee that you can probably negotiate on.

Processing or Admin Fees

It is almost universal that you will see some type of flat administration fee. It's often called a processing, underwriting, or administration fee. These range from about $500 to several thousand. This is obviously an additional revenue source for the lender and never comes up when talking terms. When a hard-money lender quotes pricing, they mention the points they charge, the interest rate, and the amount of time you can use the money. Rarely will they mention their admin fee unless asked. This again is something you will see in a term sheet or fee disclosure.

Exit Fees

I know several lenders that charge exit fees. An exit fee is paid in points when the loan pays off. Borrowers seem to like this because they are most concerned with the amount of money they need to close, which the origination fee will affect, and less with the total cost of the loan. Since the exit fee does not show up on the settlement statement and does not require any additional cash to close, many borrowers allow it or at least don't think about it. If the cost of the loan is within your budget and competitive in the market, it is OK to pay these fees, but don't be fooled into paying more than needed just because you can delay paying it.

Minimum Interest

This, too, is common with lenders. This just means that no matter how long you have the loan, you will need to pay a certain amount of interest. It is common to see three to four months of minimum interest with some hard-money lenders. So if your loan terms have a three-month minimum interest and you are able to pay your loan off in two, you will still owe a third month of interest. Depending on how this is collected, it may not show up on the settlement statement, making it hard to identify.

Application Fees

Some lenders or private-money loan brokers will charge an up-front fee to apply for the loan. Others may charge this fee after they tell you that you are formally approved for the loan. On the surface and from the lender's perspective, this can make a bit of sense. The hard-money lender is doing work to approve you and approve your deal. Some real estate investors shop for the best loan, so it is possible, and actually quite common, that a real estate investor will lead a lender on and decide not to close with them at the last minute. In these cases, the lender put in considerable effort to get ready for closing just to learn the borrower will be going with another lender. Be careful with this if you are shopping for the best rates and terms. It is much better to be transparent that you are shopping rather than pulling a loan. Pulling it will damage the relationship, and the lender may not consider lending to you in the future. Because this does happen, some hard-money lenders have started charging a fee up front to get the process started and protect themselves from the sneaky investor.

Although I understand the lender's position, I would never recommend going with a lender that charges an up-front fee. Actual costs such as inspections and appraisals are OK to pay up front but never a lender fee. Lenders' fees should be charged only when the deal closes. The reason I feel strongly about this is that there are some lenders that charge an up-front fee and never perform. They charge borrowers' fees and then don't do the loan and keep the money.

I was working with a team to develop some land in a suburb of Denver. This was an 80-acre development that included houses, a small apartment, and 10 acres of retail. I was brought in to help raise some private capital. The current management had a preapproval from a lender and just needed to hit a liquidity requirement. I decided to help and brought in a small group of investors to inject

$1 million into the project. We hit all the lender requirements, but the loan never closed. I later learned that the developer gave the lender $100,000 in a deposit for diligence and an application fee. This was a gigantic blow to the developer. He became desperate and started using the money I injected to pay personal bills. As soon as I discovered this, I took over the project and stripped the developer of all control. The bad news is that I was not a developer and did not want to be one. The good news is I learned a lot. The most important lesson, of course, was to not give a lender an application fee. That was well over a decade ago, and I still remember it clear as day. Since that time, I have seen many investors get burned by lenders with application fees. In fact, one poor lady just called our office the day I am writing this. She put $10,000 down to a wholesaler, nonrefundable, and promised to close by a certain date. She had a national hard-money lender lined up that backed out the day of closing. She gave that hard-money lender $17,000 up front in a fee to do the loan. Of course, the loan did not close, and the lender went silent. She is out $27,000 and cannot close on the deal. She called us asking us to help her close but had to close within hours. We can close in a day or two but not an hour or two. Don't pay your hard-money lender until they get you to the closing table!

With the exception of application fees, I am not saying any of these fees are good or bad; I am just saying it is wise to understand them so you know the true cost of a loan. That makes it easier for you to project your profits and also ensures that you are getting the best hard-money loan for your situation and goals.

As you can see, hard money is expensive. No matter where you get your hard-money loan, it will be more expensive than a loan from a bank or conventional lender. When looking at your numbers on a deal, you will find that behind the purchase and rehab, loan fees and interest will likely be your largest expenses.

WHY DO INVESTORS USE IT?

I get this question all the time. This question comes from both our hard-money borrowers and potential money investors of ours. Because we raise the money we loan out from individual investors, they will often ask why a real estate investor would ever pay such high rates. It is a great question because, as we know, hard money has a bad reputation, and as we mentioned, it is very expensive. Here are some of the reasons real estate investors use hard-money loans in their business.

Low Down Payment

Most hard-money lenders will require some type of down payment, but those down payments are much lower than a bank would require. If you find a good local hard-money lender, there is a chance that they will fund 100 percent of the deal and require no down payment. That is because local lenders have a great understanding of the market and the area, and they have resources to help them if they have a problem. As long as they feel they are at a good loan-to-value with the collateral, they may fund your entire project.

Obviously, there are many benefits to lower down payment requirements.

Higher ROI. Return on investment increases significantly with a smaller investment, even if it means you make a little less on a deal. We will go into more detail with case studies later, but for now, trust me: assuming you are doing profitable deals, your returns are much higher with hard-money loans.

Opportunity to scale. Hard money is not only for underqualified borrowers. Most of my clients—and, from what I hear, most hard-money borrowers—qualify for conventional and bank financing. They want to use hard money because it allows them to do more deals and make more money. As long as you are profitable and have a source for deals, you can easily make up for the costs of hard-money loans with the chance to do more deals.

I have a very successful client who uses hard money only when needed. He has significant cash reserves and income and will lean on that to fund his projects. Every once in a while, however, he hits a comfort threshold for money in the bank and shifts to funding deals with hard money to stay liquid. We supplement his thriving fix-and-flip business only when he needs it. We are the backup plan that allows him to scale.

Less risk. Although I don't necessarily agree with this, some investors will say that the less money they have in a deal, the less financial risk they are taking. It is true that the lender takes on more of the risk with a smaller down payment requirement, but be careful with this line of thinking because many hard-money lenders will require personal guarantees, and you may be liable for any loss they take.

Ease of entry. If you are getting started in your real estate investing career, maybe you don't have enough cash for the down payment. If that is the case, a hard-money lender can potentially help with your first handful of deals until you can build up your savings. Who knows? After you start a relationship with a hard-money lender, you may decide to borrow from them, even after you have the down payment a bank would require. You cannot win a game if you are not playing. Hard money is a great way to get into the game.

The House Needs Work

This is another extremely common reason to consider hard money. I was within my first two years as a hard-money lender when this one really came into focus. I received a call from a mortgage broker who had just had a deal fall apart. He wanted to know if I could help. The issue is that most banks and conventional lenders need a house to be habitable for them to fund it. The term "habitability" can be somewhat broad and is dependent on someone's opinion in many cases, but one thing that seems to be consistent is that the house needs at least one conforming bedroom (or sleeping area for a studio). In this example the house had no bedrooms. The reason? No closets.

This was going to be a great rental property for his client, but he was denied his loan. He had the down payment, the income, and the credit to qualify but could not get to the closing table. The mortgage broker was beside himself and had no control and no solutions. He found us online and, out of desperation, gave us a call. The subject property was a foreclosure, and the prior occupant had some fun with what appeared to be a sledgehammer. I guess he or she was upset that the bank wanted to foreclose for not getting any payments. Many walls were damaged, including the closets in the bedrooms. In fact, there were no functional closets, which is why the appraiser marketed it as not habitable. At that time, you could finish off a closet for about $500, which the investor planned to do after he closed on his purchase. Because of a simple $500 repair that was still necessary, he was denied.

Luckily, we were able to step in and fund the purchase, and we funded some of the repair money. He was able to do more improvements than he originally planned, making the house better. He made the repairs, got a new appraisal, and refinanced us with the same mortgage broker. The mortgage broker won because he helped his client and still was able to do a loan for him; the client won because he was able to purchase and repair the house and it took a lot less of his money to do it; and we won because we made a great loan that was paid off in a few short months. This is the perfect example of a win-win-win situation. This was a huge eye-opening transaction for me. Shortly after this experience, we started funding many buyers wanting to buy rentals. This strategy allowed them to buy properties with very little or even no money down. This strategy was later coined (not by us) "BRRRR," which we discuss in great detail later in the book.

Speed

Hard-money lenders can close in days, not months. That is a huge advantage to professional real estate investors for many reasons.

More competitive offers. Whenever a seller accepts an offer and changes the MLS listing to "Pending" or "Under contract," they are taking a risk. If a house hits the market, goes under contract, and then comes back on the market, it will have a negative stigma. It is automatically assumed that there is something wrong with the house, even if there is not. This perceived problem lessens the value. As we all know, perception is reality. A house will usually sell for less on a second or third contract than it did with the first, so an accepted offer that does not close diminishes value. That is risk. In fact, some real estate investors target these homes and come in with lowball offers. Good real estate agents and Realtors know this, which is why they want a preapproval letter, and the really good agents will vet the buyer by calling the lender and asking targeted questions. If a house hits the market and the seller receives two offers, one with a 45-day close and one with a seven-day close, all things being equal, they will take the seven days. That is obvious, but how much of a discount will it take to close in seven days instead of 45? Your offer can compete with speed instead of price in some cases, which means you can potentially get better deals.

It is also important to be competitive in a competitive market. When real estate is tight—meaning more buyers than houses—

sellers often will not even consider on offer that is not cash or a fast close with a solid loan. To even be in consideration, you need to close fast.

Backup offers. I cannot count the number of times that a buyer backed out of a deal and one of my clients got the deal. The call comes in: "Kevin, can you get me closed by the end of the week?" It is not that they are writing formal backup offers, but they are networking and letting people know they can close fast. The reason they can close fast is, of course, hard money. A fantastic strategy to get deals is to network with Realtors, title companies, conventional lenders, attorneys, and anyone else involved in closings and let them know what you are looking for. The more people you tell and who get to know you, the greater the chance someone will call when a closing falls apart.

I know Realtors who are so dedicated to finding deals for their investor clients that they call the listing agents on deals that are under contract. They call simply to let the agent know that if the deal falls apart for any reason, they have a buyer interested. These are deals that fit their investors' criteria. These are probably dilapidated houses or properties that can be improved in some way, which is great because those are the properties that are more likely to fall out of contract. If you are a motivated agent, this is a great strategy to find deals for your clients. It is nice for the listing agent to call their seller with news that the contract is falling apart when they have a replacement buyer ready to close in a week or less.

If you are a real estate investor who is willing to look for and find deals that are not listed in the MLS, this will become a giant benefit in your business. As you are marketing for off-market properties, you will be meeting many motivated sellers. Not all sellers will be ready to pull the trigger on the day you speak to them, or they may not like or understand your below-market offer. As time goes on, the pain that is motivating them could intensify, and they may decide that selling to you is their best option. Knowing they can call you and get the deal closed in a week releases stress from their lives. You will find that as long as you were able to build rapport when you met them and have some sort of system to stay in touch, you can use hard money and quick closes to get more deals!

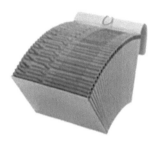

Although I still invest in real estate on a regular basis, I no longer have the time to market for and meet with sellers about buying their property. My focus is now on raising capital and helping other investors with their success by funding their deals. With that said, I was an investor first, and when I was getting started in the world of real estate, I found almost 100 percent of my deals off-market. I had a full marketing system that included cold calls, signs, mailings, ads, and flyers. As seller leads came in, I tracked them with a sophisticated follow-up system. I completed a seller intake form—I called it a seller call sheet—for each call I received. This form included the seller's name, contact information, how they heard about me, basic property information, and seller motivation. I also included a spot for notes. This was my customer relationship management (CRM) system: some sheets of paper and a pen. I also had one of those old accordion folders with 31 slots, one for each day of the month. If I did not set an appointment to meet the seller at their home and I sensed a hint of motivation, I stuck my seller call sheet in the accordion file for a few days later. For example, if I took a call from a seller and there was a reason for motivation, such as a job transfer or divorce, on the fifth of the month, I would stash the call sheet in the slot for the eighth or ninth. Each day that I made calls, I picked out all the files for that day and made those calls first. On the eighth day of the month, I would just call and check in and see how their process was going and remind them I could close in a week. If I still did not get the appointment, I would file the call sheet again for several days later. I continued this until they either asked me to stop or they sold their house. I used this same system when I made offers on houses that were not accepted. If there was any sense of motivation, I kept calling them until they either worked with me or got their problem solved somewhere else. In my experience, once you meet with a motivated seller, they do not get upset at the follow-up. In fact, they tend to really appreciate it. Although they may not see you as their best option at the time, you are an option, nonetheless.

There are many much better CRM systems out there today than some paper and an accordion file. Salesforce and HubSpot tend to lead the pack, but any system that allows you to take notes and set tasks to follow up on will work. Most have a free version that will be more than enough, so there is no need to fork out any cash to get started.

Sometimes a seller will fall out of your system and still call you down the road to accept an offer. Many years ago, I was looking at a small apartment building in Missouri. This property had some challenges that made it a perfect target for a value-add investor. The sellers were an elderly couple, and the husband was ill and would be needing care. His wife was not able to manage the property on her own. Everything on paper looked great, and we basically had a deal in place. I just wanted to see the property and finish up the details of the negotiation in person. I flew out there and discovered that there were two fewer units than what was disclosed. One unit was being used as the community laundry center, and one was owner storage. I saw the laundry income on the financials but did not understand that it was located in what used to be one of the units. This was a medium-stay rental building, which meant rental terms from several weeks to several months. Every unit was fully furnished, so the storage space was essential. Once I discovered this, the upside on the deal changed, and the numbers as discussed no longer worked. I had to get a better price. After I explained my position and the price I was willing to pay, the seller was no longer willing to sell. We just could not come to terms. I flew home disappointed and relieved that I discovered the issue. I followed up a handful of times, but they were not motivated, so I wished them well and tossed my call sheet in the recycle bin. More than a year later, they called and asked me if my offer was still good. They could not get their price because it was not worth what they wanted. Their motivation had grown. My diligence was mostly done; I just needed to verify what I knew and line up my nonbank "can close fast" lender, and we closed a week later.

Backup funding. As a hard-money lender, I hate putting this in here. At times I feel like the ugly guy in the club or at the party. Investors come talk to me when their other options have gone home with someone else. It is common for real estate investors to fall back on hard money when they run out of time. What I mean by that is they negotiate a deal with a typical close timeline, like thirty or forty days. They then start looking for the money. That's when they hit trouble. Maybe it is a bank that cannot close on time (banks can take forever), or they need to raise the down payment and can't get the commitments. I could probably write an entire book on problems that blow up closings, and 85 percent of that book would be financing. Financing falls apart for many, many reasons. A good hard-money lender has your back. If you have the relationship and a good deal, they will go to bat for you. They will push what is on their desk aside and get you closed. No hard-money lender wants to be the only option when the bar announces last call, but they all understand it.

With all this said, I do want to mention that we get calls several times a month from new clients wanting a quick close. Like "a few days" quick. If we have not done business or do not know someone and they call out of the blue wanting a quick close, the answer is probably no. *But* if we have done deals together and gotten to know each other, the chances of a yes are very high. Many hard-money lenders can close a deal in one or two days if they have the relationship. This is very different from other types of loans. Relationships matter!

Short sales. There was a time when short sales were extremely popular, and I would expect that they will come back at some point. A short sale is a lender accepting less than what is owed on the loan to release the lien, which enables the borrower to sell the house when they have little to no equity. This was very common in the credit crash of 2008, when many homes were underwater, but is a strategy used by investors in all market conditions.

Before I started lending private money in 2006, I was working for Wall Street companies as a mortgage bond analyst. In the conventional world, mortgages would get packaged up with hundreds and sometimes thousands of other mortgages and sold on Wall Street as a mortgage bond. These bonds were attractive to investors because they came with a fixed rate of return and felt safe because they were backed by American real estate. What could go wrong? These mortgage bonds fed Wall Street greed, which was a major factor in the crash of 2008. You don't see as many of these bonds out there today, but they do exist. Now we see Fannie Mae and Freddie Mac buying most of these loans. The process remains the same. You have loan originators, loan servicers, and the owners of the loans. For example, Wells Fargo does all three, but mostly they originate and service the loans then sell many of them to Fannie Mae or Freddie Mac. They and other originators do this to free up their capital to make more loans. They make money on origination and servicing fees, not interest. In this example you would make your payment to Wells Fargo, but other than a small fee, the money would go to Fannie Mae, Freddie Mac, or whoever owns the loan. Loan servicers are graded on how well they do, so it is important to them to reduce losses as much as possible. And they have analysts like me poking around, asking why losses were taken on specific loans.

On top of all these reasons to liquidate nonperforming loans, many people don't understand that servicers are often required to send payments to the owners of the loans, even if they are not receiving payments from the borrowers. This was a big concern during the COVID-19 pandemic, as the government stopped loan servicers' ability to collect on defaulted loans by mandating forbearance agreements and stopping foreclosures, but they expected servicers to continue the payments to Fannie Mae and Freddie Mac. This requirement is what creates the fixed income on these securities and is even more of a reason to get these nonperforming loans off the books.

I learned as an analyst that the owners of conventional loans take tremendous losses when their loans go all the way through the foreclosure process. On average, losses on loans that make it through the foreclosure process and become bank owned are close to 50 percent. Or at least it was when I was analyzing these bonds. That is a huge loss and a major incentive to get these loans off the books. Since servicers are graded on loan defaults and losses, they are willing to work with real estate investors to accept less than what is owed on the loans to allow the seller to sell the home. A short sale is a tool that allows loan servicers to take a smaller loss now and move on rather than keeping nonperforming loans on the books with the chance of a much larger loss later. Sometimes the loan servicer will ask the owner to pay the balance of what remains unpaid, but most of the time, they will just write it off as a loss. This is one strategy that real estate investors use to create equity in homes they are buying.

The problem with short sales, especially when there are a lot of foreclosures, is they can take a while to put together. There is normally a checklist of items the loan servicer is going to need, including a listing agreement, borrower financials, hardship letters, net sheets or settlement statements, and a valuation. This is known as the short sale package. The lender will most likely also order their own valuation. Often, items from the package will get misplaced or lost, so the investor needs to stay on top of this. This process can take months, but once the approval comes in, the window to close the transaction can be very short. I have seen closings scheduled within one week after the short sale approval comes in, but getting that approval took six months. These short timelines require a lender that can move fast!

Timing with construction crews. When you have a construction crew that you like, you will be motivated to work around their schedule. They will not wait around for you to close on a house; they will take another job if they can. Downtime costs them money. If you have a crew that can start, but it is before you are scheduled to close on the house, you can move the closing sooner with a lender that can close fast so you don't lose your crew.

The timing of construction draws is also extremely important to keep your crews happy. Hard-money lenders are far faster at approving and releasing draws, so you can keep your crews paid and happy.

Ease of Underwriting

The thing about banks and conventional lenders is you need to fit into their little box, or you will be denied. It is extremely rare for these lenders to consider an exception with compensating factors and approve a loan if even one requirement is not met. Here are some of the basic requirements for a single-family home that you would need to fit into to qualify for conventional loans. These get even more restrictive if you do a deal on anything more than a single-family, like a two-, three-, or four-unit building.

Credit. At the time I wrote this, the credit score requirement for a non-owner-occupied loan, an investment loan, is 640. The lender pulls what they call a tri-merge credit report, which merges all three credit bureau reports—Experian, Equifax, and Transunion—together. This report also gives you the credit scores from all three. The lender considers only the score in the middle of the three. With anything less than a 640, you are denied.

Down payment. We have started to see this loosen a bit, but as a general rule, banks and conventional lenders will want to see a minimum of 20 percent down. It is possible to get loans at 15 percent down, but those are harder to get and require mortgage insurance. Mortgage insurance is paid monthly and added to your loan, so you will have a higher rate with the added insurance premium. Keep in mind that you will need to cover the 20 percent down payment, the closings costs, and any needed repairs to get the deal done. And after all that, you will need to show that you have enough reserves to still qualify.

Cash. Lenders will require that you have reserves. This will be the money you have in liquid accounts after you pay your down payment and your costs to close. As long as you have four financed properties or fewer, your reserve requirement will be two percent of the total amount of your unpaid principal balance on all your loans. This number jumps to four percent of total principal balance from five properties to six, and finally all the way to six percent with more than six properties. So if you are financing your seventh property, and all your loans are $200,000, your total reserves requirement would be $84,000: $200,000 times seven loans times six percent. A more recent change that does help borrowers is that now 100 percent of your retirement account can be used to meet this requirement. Any of these guidelines can change at any time.

Keep in mind that this requirement is after you close. To get the deal done, you will need to show that you have your down payment, your closing costs, *and* your reserve requirement.

Debt compared with income. When making a loan decision, the lender will look at a debt-to-income ratio, or DTI. This tells them if you make enough money to support the monthly payments. The ratio is calculated by taking your monthly payments on all your debt, including the new loan payment, other mortgages, car loans, credit cards, and anything else you are paying on that is considered debt, and dividing that by your monthly income before taxes. Basically, they look at how much of your income is being used to make payments on debt. When buying a rental property, they will consider the rent in your income.

The maximum DTI is 36 percent, but there are exceptions up to 45 percent for factors such as higher credit and reserves. If you are over these limits, your loan will be denied.

Loan amount limits. It is rare to see this as a problem for investment properties, but conventional lenders have maximum loan limits. Because the most expensive homes do not cash flow as well, you do not usually see investors hit these limits. The limit for a single-family home is $548,250 and will go up if the property has more than one unit or is in a high-cost area.

Number of loan limits. This guideline is often misunderstood. You are actually able to finance as many as ten properties, not four, as many believe. The problem is that even though Fannie Mae allows it, many lenders will cut you off at four. If you run into that, call around because you might find another lender to do it. It is also important to know that guidelines tighten after your fourth property. We already discussed the increase in cash reserves, but your down payment requirement will increase, and so will your minimum credit score. In fact, the credit requirement jumps all the way to 720 after your fourth property.

As a reminder, these guidelines are constantly changing and probably have changed between the time I wrote this and when you are reading it. Despite any potential changes to the guidelines in the future, I shared these so you can see how restrictive conventional lenders can be.

You can see that you have to be a pretty well qualified borrower to use conventional loans, especially if you already own a handful of rentals. This is just one more reason to consider hard money.

Draws

A draw is when the lender issues a portion of the loan to the borrower to pay for construction or improvements. It is very common if you are borrowing the money to rehab a house that the lender will want to do inspections and issue draws as work is complete. Banks and private-money lenders often take weeks to get a draw out. A good hard-money operation has a team in place to process these and can get draws out fast. As we have discussed, fast draws are important because your contractors want to get paid, and you want them to work.

Cheaper Than a Partner

I have had clients complain to me about our fees and interest and decide not to borrow but instead bring in a partner to help with the down payment so they can get a bank loan. They agree to share a portion of the deal with the partner to compensate them for their investment. If you are doing profitable deals, giving a share of the upside to a partner is probably more expensive than what you would pay a hard-money lender. Because many hard-money lenders have smaller down payment requirements, you may be able to eliminate the need for a partner. I suggest you run the numbers both ways before you commit to giving up some of your deal, and I bet you'll find that hard money is a far superior option.

I have a longtime client and friend who does business in Minneapolis. He is an outstanding investor and a better human. He built his successful business by bringing in partners to fund down payments and construction costs and fix-and-flip residential houses. That was before he met me, though. Once we started working together, he was able to eliminate the need for partners and added personal profits on every deal he does. Since then, he has grown to be one of the largest and most-respected investors in the city. He has a big team and now has shifted his focus to commercial value-added projects. He still runs a large fix-and-flip business and now added hard-money bridge loans to his arsenal; he is doing much larger, much more profitable projects.

As you can see, there are many reasons investors choose to use hard-money financing. This is why we have clients come back over and over again and why they are happy to refer us to their investor friends. Hard money is only one tool in your tool belt, but it is nice to have the right tool when you need it. If you run into a situation that requires a flexible and fast source of cash, hard money just flat works!

Chapter 2

Fix-and-Flips

When I got started lending private money in 2006, I funded only fix-and-flips. This is what I understood, and it was the primary reason investors used hard money back then. Although we have expanded to many other financing tools, fix-and-flip loans continue to be the most common reason real estate investors borrow from us. Hard money really does work well for the fix-and-flip investor.

You have probably seen the popular television shows about making money fixing and flipping homes. Buy a beat-up house for cheap, remodel it, and resell it for huge profits. I will admit that those shows are highly entertaining, which is why they have done so well, and although they are not accurate to the real-life business, they do a great job getting viewers excited about fixing and flipping houses.

It was my third deal as a real estate investor. I had already converted my primary home into a rental and accomplished two no-money-down lease options when I did my first fix-and-flip. This gentleman was recently divorced and had to sell his house in Arvada, Colorado, fast! I had a full marketing campaign that included direct mail to sellers I thought would be motivated and signs in areas of town I wanted to buy in. These are the "We Buy Houses" signs you see on the side of the road. I would hang twenty-five signs every Friday night. It is so funny looking back on those darn signs. I would dress in all black and try to be as stealthy as possible. I guess I was embarrassed to be pounding a stake into the ground to staple a sign to. I did not enjoy hanging those signs, but they worked! It was a sign that prompted the call from this motivated seller. We met in his living room and negotiated the deal. I bought the house for $150,000, and I thought it would sell for $210,000. If the house needed much rehab, those numbers would not have worked, but all it needed were some minor repairs, paint, carpet, and a good cleaning. I did most of the work and had it sold in no time. We did not use a Realtor and my partner provided most of the money. I made my first $17,000 as a real estate investor.

Fix-and-flips can come in different shapes and sizes. I have done fix-and-flips where we added square footage and some where it was as simple as some carpet and paint, like my deal in Arvada. We have clients doing simple cosmetic remodels, and we have some reconfiguring floor plans, digging out basements, splitting off a lot, or using a number of other creative strategies.

FIND THE FLIP

This is a popular topic and one that has received a ton of attention from real estate gurus. Without a deal, well, there is no deal. You as a real estate investor will need to learn how to locate your projects. The best investors we work with find deals on the multiple listing service (MLS), through other investors, or through their own marketing. Ideally you will want sellers calling you asking you to buy their house. This is the best way to find killer deals because you may be the only investor speaking with that seller, like I was on my first deal in Arvada. Be sure to subscribe to our newsletter and subscribe to our YouTube channel, which are both packed with useful information for real estate investors, including specific strategies we know are working to help you find your next project.

Find us on YouTube at or sign up for our newsletter or check out other resources at www.fundyourflip.com.

FUND THE FLIP

Once you locate the property that will be profitable, you will need to learn how to finance it. There are many ways that investors finance their projects.

Conventional Loans

We have already discussed some of the restrictions of conventional loans. These loans are so prevalent that I wanted to go into more detail about using them specifically for fix-and-flips.

Conventional loans will be the cheapest money you find. A conventional loan is any loan purchased by Fannie Mae or Freddie Mac. Fannie and Freddie are the two government entities that help create liquidity in the market. They do this by buying loans from lenders. In order for a lender to sell a loan to one of these mortgage giants, they need to be sure that the loan falls within the conventional loan guidelines. It is very important for conventional loan originators to sell their loans so they can free up their cash to make more loans and charge more fees. If they cannot sell the loans, they will go out of business. This is why they are so strict with the guidelines.

Because Fannie and Freddie have unlimited funds and will buy everything that fits the guidelines, the prices are low. Unlimited supply will drive down the price. For that reason, I would say use as much of this cheap money as you can in your real estate business, especially on rental homes, but conventional loans have their downsides for fix-and-flip investors.

Down payment requirement. As previously discussed, one of the guidelines that must be met by the fix-and-flip investor is the amount of down payment requirement to purchase an investment home. As of today, when I write this, the down payment requirement is 20 percent without the additional cost of mortgage insurance.

Funding the construction. Conventional lenders will not fund any construction on investment homes. So to use a conventional loan for your fix-and-flip, you will need to fund the down payment *and* all of the construction costs. This could be a significant amount of your own cash into each deal.

No short-term funding. Fannie and Freddie are in this for a profit. And they have investors expecting returns. What I think is important to understand is that these loans are not profitable for the first several years. The loan originator is the only one to make a profit because they charge fees. Conventional lenders make money on interest, not fees. For this reason, they want the loans to last a long time, and it hurts them when they don't. There were many changes and restrictions on loans after the crash in 2008, including the ability for lenders to add prepayment penalties to loans. A prepayment penalty is a fee to the borrower if they pay off the loan within a set amount of time. This penalty helped ensure the lender would be profitable, even if the loan paid off early. Now there are restrictions on prepayment penalties, so lenders have other strategies to help ensure profit. Often, they will require originators to refund fees or their profits in deals that pay off early. This can become a big problem for your bank or mortgage broker, so let them know your plan is to fix and flip, if that is, in fact, your plan. If too many loans pay off early, your lender may have to stop lending to you.

Bank Loans

Bank loans can be great ways to fund fix-and-flips. Although more expensive than a conventional lender, they will be far cheaper than other funding options, and some are OK with the shorter nature of fix-and-flip loans. Usually, if you are going to go this route, you will want to focus on the smaller commercial or community banks. These are the ones with a handful of branches with whom you can build a personal relationship. Many of these banks hold on to the loans they originate. We call these "portfolio lenders" because they keep their loans in their portfolio instead of selling them off. Portfolio lenders often want shorter-term loans. In fact, it is very common to see maturity dates or balloon dates on these loans, forcing the borrower to pay them off with a lump sum payment before the end of the full term. A loan balloon means that the entire amount of the loan is due on that date. So although your loan payments might be based on a 25 or 30 year amortization, it will likely be due in three to five years. Because these banks portfolio their loans, they do not have to stick to the normal conventional guidelines. This is huge for investors for many reasons, but for fix-and-flip investors, this means they can potentially help fund the rehab, and they can look past common conventional roadblocks such as lack of documented income or a lower credit score.

Of course, there are a few downsides to borrowing from banks.

Down payments. Banks tend to be pretty conservative, even more so than conventional lenders in some cases. While you can get loan amounts from conventional lenders at 80 percent or even 85 percent of the purchase, you will likely be closer to 70 percent to 75 percent with banks. That ratio is based on purchase price unless they are also financing the rehab. In those cases, the 70 percent to 75 percent would be on total costs including your rehab.

Qualifying. Outside of the down payment needed, banks will have other requirements. Banks love cash flowing real estate, which a fix-and-flip is not, so right out of the gate, they may be hesitant. Cash flowing real estate is something that is rented and producing income on its own that can cover the loan payments. Because a fix-and-flip is vacant, it has no cash flow, so the bank will want to be sure you can carry the loan if needed. This is called a global DTI ratio or global cash flow. They want to see that with all your income and all your expenses, you can afford the loan. This can be extremely challenging for real estate investors because income is sporadic and investors tend to get a little creative with their tax deductions, making it difficult to prove income, not to mention that adding a vacant house with a new mortgage hurts a DTI ratio. Banks will also focus on liquidity, credit, and your relationship with them.

Time. Banks are notorious for being slow. Like, really slow! It is not uncommon for a bank to take six weeks to approve a loan. Conventional lenders often approve loans with an automated process. That just means that a computer approves the loan, and the underwriter just verifies that all the data entered was accurate. They do this by checking bank statements, tax returns, and other documents. Banks have a very different and much more manual process to approve loans. Banks like to talk about loans, so they have the loan officer, often called a vice president, put the loan together and then present it to a committee that will approve or deny the loan. The committee meets once or twice a week, so it is not like you can get a quick answer. And if there are questions on your loan, it will need to go back to the committee once those questions are answered.

Bankers speak. "Greenspan speak" is a term for answering a question without answering it. Politicians are fantastic at this. This is something I never got very good at, but I remember learning this skill in Toastmasters. The exercise was to answer a simple question but talk for two minutes. Sounds easy right? The first time I had to do this, the question was "If you could have any superpower, what would it be?" I remember this so clearly because I was scared to death! I told them the question reminded me of the Adam Sandler movie *Click* and then froze. I literally stood there without saying a word for about ninety seconds. That is a long damn time when a room of about twenty professionals are staring at you without being able to help at all. I could not sleep that night and thought maybe that would be my last Toastmasters event. The only way to succeed with this Toastmasters staple exercise is to talk about something that may be related but is not answering the question at all, maybe by telling a story you want your audience to hear. It might start with, "That question reminds me of a time…" And away you go. I did go back to Toastmasters after this embarrassing failure, and I did get better at this exercise by not answering the question at all. I knew the story I wanted to share, no matter what the question was.

Alan Greenspan was an absolute pro at telling you what you wanted to hear. Not much of what he said was true, but you sure believed it when he said it. Greenspan was the chair of the Federal Reserve when I was getting started in the mortgage industry. I remember learning the term "Greenspan speak" from my mentor, Joe. He told me that Alan had to be so incredibly careful because his words affected the entire economy. OK, maybe I can understand why Greenspan would tell the media what he thought the people wanted to hear, but what about your banker who cannot shoot you straight?

I believe that it is important to understand the banking industry, at least on the surface, as a real estate investor. Bankers you will run into with your real estate investing will almost all be vice presidents. Some will have other fancy names. Vice president bankers are the ones who are out there trying to stir up business for the bank. They are the ones you get transferred to if you call or who will come out and say hi if you drop in at a branch. Their job is to sell the bank. They want your business, so many of them will tell you what you want to hear, much like Greenspan, and not always what you should hear.

As real estate investors, we rely on funding to operate. If your funding is your bank, just be careful you are getting the straight story and that they will actually come through for you. It is important to understand that the mere fact that their business card reads "vice president" does not mean they are second in line to a president. They more than likely are great salespeople and can possibly help you, but do not make the mistake of believing that they are the ones who make, or even help make, credit decisions. They may not even be in the room when credit decisions are made. I share this with you only to protect you from falling for the banker telling you what you want to hear. Dig in a little to see who is making the decision and what they are looking for, and always have a plan B. Hard-money lenders are a fantastic plan B, and most of them will tell you the truth right out of the gate. And you can actually talk to the person making the decision on the loan. They can also close fast, so build that relationship just in case your banker lets you down.

I am not saying don't borrow from banks. Far from it. In fact, bankers can be one of your most important allies in this business. Let's face it. You need money, and they have it. I am simply saying to be careful believing what they tell you.

I have pretty good relationships with a handful of banks. Multiple relationships are important. I had a deal I needed to close quickly. We had to bring in a decent amount of funds to get it done. I requested help from two different banks, and thank God I did. We got the deal closed because one of my relationships came through. The other one told me twice it was not going to be an issue and even went so far as to say they were excited to be doing this deal together. Two weeks later, the vice president told me his credit committee shot down the deal. After two weeks of me being told "no issues," the rug was pulled. Understanding how the bank works saved me here. I knew this was a creative loan and it was possible it would be rejected, so I planned for that. Banks need to stay within their box, so I am not upset they did not do the deal. I am disappointed they told me they could do it when they couldn't, even though I know this is the game. Although this was not my first rodeo, it is an important reminder to have backup plans, especially when there are significant profits on the line.

It is going to be hard to trust this bank or this specific banker's "banker speak" ever again.

Owner Carry

Owner carry is a creative and effective way to finance real estate. It is when you are able to buy a property and have the owner carry some or all of the purchase in a loan, acting as the bank. Because it is the owner and not a bank, you can get creative with the terms.

When I was starting out, I had no money and very little credit. I also did not have much in the way of income. I had a job and was getting paid some from the GI Bill from my military service, but I was a 21-year-old full time student. I would not qualify for conventional or bank loans, so I had to get creative. Before I learned about hard money, I learned how to structure no-money-down deals with sellers. I would purchase one or two houses a month without down payments or credit applications. That experience taught me a lot and forced my creativity as I progressed through my career.

Owner carry does not always mean the owner carries the entire amount. It could be they own the property free and clear and carry the full amount, or it could mean they carry a second mortgage, reducing the amount you give them up front. It really can mean anything that you and the seller can come up with that works for both of you.

The most common owner-carry structures are detailed in the graphic below.

Column A shows the 100 percent financing from the sellers. This is what I got good at when I was purchasing a deal or two a month. There are several ways to accomplish this, including *lease options, subject to, contract for deed, wraparound mortgage,* and a *simple note and mortgage* or *deed of trust.*

Column B is identical to column A but is when the seller wants you to have a down payment. For this example, the seller will carry all of the purchase, but you would need to put five percent down.

Column C is when you are funding with a bank and need to meet the bank's down payment requirement. In this example, the seller covers your down payment for you with a loan. They will most likely record a deed of trust or mortgage, so this is commonly referred to as a second mortgage.

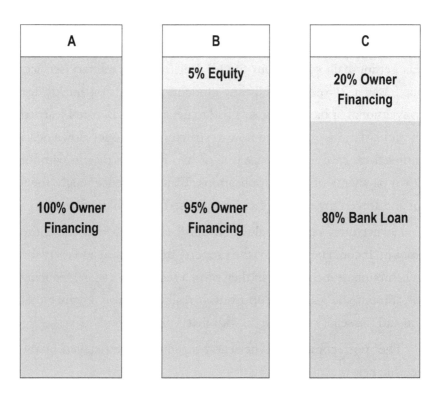

The one thing all three of these examples have in common is that you will need to fund the repairs yourself. These are just examples of how you may be able to purchase the property.

Two years ago, I saw a client do one of the most creative no-money-down transactions I have seen. He negotiated with a seller to keep some of the seller's equity in the deal for a piece of the profit. This enabled my client to get a bank loan and use the current owner's equity as the equity requirement, so he did not have to put any of his money into the deal. He got in with nothing down simply by sharing a piece of the upside with the seller. This strategy might not work so well with residential properties, especially if you are trying to finance it with a conventional loan, but it easily works in the commercial space. Some kind of owner participation is one of my all-time favorite ways to finance real estate, but it, too, has some downsides:

Hard to find and negotiate. In residential real estate, it is rare to see any type of creativity when working with listing agents. So if the property is listed for sale in the MLS, you will need to negotiate through an agent, making it challenging to get a deal done. There are several reasons for this. First, agents don't learn these creative deal structures, so their lack of understanding is uncomfortable and makes it difficult to explain and sell to their client. Another reason is that many motivated sellers who would be open to these strategies don't have the money to pay their agent. They need the money from the sale of the real estate to pay the commission. Agents, from my experience, have no interest in selling real estate without a clear commission. Finally, many times, it takes you, the investor, the one making the offer, to build the rapport to get the seller to feel comfortable. You cannot usually do that through an agent. It takes meeting in person and, many times, several follow-ups or multiple meetings to build that relationship. I have purchased a handful of houses that were listed with an agent. I was only able to accomplish that by having a meeting with the seller while the agent was present. We had to negotiate the deal and negotiate a separate deal to be sure the agent was paid. Some of those were me paying it, and some were paying it over time with income from the property.

Because it is unlikely that you will have success negotiating a seller carry with an agent involved, the best way to find these types of structures is off-market. We are talking about beat-up, outdated houses that are candidates for fixing and flipping, so most investors look for financial distress. The most common and obvious are foreclosures. It normally starts with getting the foreclosure list, which is available through most title companies, and then working the list. You can also use cold calls, knocking on doors, or the most common: sending them letters in the mail. These are the sellers who are losing their houses to foreclosure, so they are likely to be in a desperate situation with which you can help. Because their motivation is so high, they are more likely to be open to creative strategies to solve their problem. This is one fantastic source of potential owner-carry deals, but any time you can get in front of a seller directly, there is an opportunity for a creative solution. However, finding off-market deals takes time, hard work, and often money for marketing.

May not fund repairs. Depending on how you structure your owner-carry deal, there may not be money for the repairs. If the owner is carrying a second mortgage, for example, and you plan to use a bank for the primary funding, the bank most likely will not also fund repairs knowing there is another loan on the property. Unless you are using hard or private money in the funding stack, I am not sure how you would fund repairs with an owner carry unless, of course, the owner funds the repairs. I was successful in negotiating an owner helping me fund improvements only one time in the thousands of deals I have been part of. This may be one of my own personal limiting beliefs, but I find that it is extremely unlikely because if the owner has the money to fund the repairs, they probably would have made the repairs themselves. The one time I was successful with this was when we were able to create the cash needed for the repairs through the sale of the house, and then the owner loaned me the money in a separate transaction that I repaid when I sold the house.

The unwanted partner. I do not have enough fingers and toes to count the number of times my clients or other real estate investors have been forced into a partnership with a toxic partner because of these deals. Owner carry is fantastic! I do absolutely love these types of creative strategies, but with them comes the seller. If your structure gives them equity and any sense of control, they may try to use that. Even if they are in debt and it is only a loan that they gave you, some sellers will be very curious about the deal and progress and will check in. I have heard stories of sellers showing up to the job site and harassing the contractors, trying to get involved with negotiations with buyers, trying to make decisions on the construction or exit strategy, and causing any number of other issues. All of this is easy to overcome with a good structure and an agreement in place, but it is a hassle and creates a challenge for the investor.

Private Lenders

Private lenders are a fantastic way to fund fix-and-flips, and if you have good relationships with investors willing to fund your deals, you should nourish those. Although I am a hard-money lender, I will admit that private-money lenders may be the single best way to fund these transactions.

Private money is exactly what it sounds like: money from private people. These are normally friends and family, people you meet at a networking event, or someone you are referred to. Because these are just individual investors, you can negotiate with them. Most will consider you a borrower and loan you money for a set interest rate. Many times, these rates are lower than hard money, which is why this is so attractive. It is also similar to hard money in that it is easier to qualify because there is no set box you are forced to fit into. As good as private money is, there are some downsides.

Thanksgiving. If you are borrowing from family and or friends and you end up losing money, Thanksgiving can get a little awkward. Whenever you do business with friends and family, you bring in a new and complex element to your investing. Relationships are easily ruined over money, especially when it is not returned, so be very careful when dealing with friends and family. The money that we loan out is privately raised, and when I started Pine Financial, I was not comfortable asking friends and family for their investment. I started by raising money from private investors I met networking or was referred to. Because I was not comfortable with accepting investments from friends and family, I focused on raising money from more sophisticated investors first. Once I proved that my process would be successful, I let my family and friends in on what I was creating. Now we have multiple private and public funds, and I have friends and family members in all of them. Now I have a high level of confidence in my ability to protect their money, so I no longer have reservations about accepting these funds. I know many real estate investors who started raising capital from friends and family and later accepted outside investors. To each their own, but be cautious and do whatever it takes to protect the money anytime you accept private capital into your deals.

Finding the money. Outside of friends and family, where do you even find the money? I had success because I would teach seminars and webinars and raised money that way. From there, I started getting referrals and meeting people at networking events. It was a hard task and took a significant amount of time and effort. For many real estate investors, their time is better spent finding deals instead of finding investors because they know how to find deals and know they have funding sources ready to go when they do.

Regulation. A promissory note is considered a security in most, if not all, states. There are regulations on selling securities without a license. Securities law is something you do not want to get caught up in. I do know that there are exemptions to a licensing requirement in some areas of the country if you are raising money for your own deals or doing a limited number of transactions, but I would still highly recommend you get a competent attorney to review your plan to be sure you stay compliant.

During my second year in this business, I was told by one of my competitors that I needed a security license with the state of Colorado. I was learning this business from my mentor, who had been doing it for years and was someone I looked up to. Susan assured me that no license was necessary. As my arrangement with her was coming to an end so we could each pursue our own career path, and the thought of starting Pine Financial was on my mind, I decided to call the state to ask them if what I was currently doing was legal. Bad idea! The response I received was an invitation to their downtown office.

There I sat, in my blue jeans and polo shirt at a table that looked like it belonged in the Donald Trump show *The Apprentice*, when I realized that this invitation was much larger than a simple meeting with a regulator.

In walked who I first thought was a professional wrestler. He must have been six-foot-six and built like a rock with a large belt, a badge, and a gun. Yes, a gun! He approached from the opposite side of the table and reached across to set his business card in front of me. He pulled out his chair and sat down as he told me his name, which you would think I would have remembered. I do remember that it started with "Investigator." This was an investigator for the state of Colorado, and he had no intention of giving me information or answering my questions. He was there to *get* information. As the shock was setting in, we sat in silence. In less than a minute, a second person I will never forget walked in. She was Cheryl Limon, with whom I've had the pleasure of working many times since this meeting. Cheryl was in charge of the mortgage broker dealers within the Colorado Department of Regulatory Agency's Division of Securities.

The meeting began. I was asked questions for several hours about my history, my current lending activities, my plans for the future, whom I knew, my investors, and pretty much everything in between. Then I was given some homework. I was forced to submit personal, professional, and financial documents for ten years of history, including the names and contact information for every borrower and every investor I had ever worked with. Talk about a peek under the skirt. I quickly learned that my competitor, Dave, was right! I did need a license, and I did not have one, and as this process progressed, I started to think that I may never get one. The stress was real. I was recently married and had a six-month-old daughter. How was I going to make a living?

It was challenging to sleep after this meeting, and the investigation took several months, which I have since learned is about record time when dealing with regulators. As much as I hated Cheryl at the time, she was actually helping me get this done fast. When it was all over, sweet Cheryl told me that I was operating at a high level, and other than getting my investors to sign disclosures, I was actually providing more detail and transparency then was even required by the state. Can you believe it? I was exceeding expectations, and I did not even know I was getting graded. She commended me for how I was doing everything and said she would be happy to consider me for the mortgage broker dealer license with the state, but I would need to file all the documents, pass the criminal background check, pass the test, and finally pay the fees. There were no required classes, so I learned what I needed online and took the test, the Series 63, and passed. Shortly after I received my license, I was back in business!

I learned a lot from this process, obviously, but the most important thing is that the regulators are not your friend. Cheryl turned out to be sweet and helped me, but she was not there to be my friend, and she started out extremely tough. I am convinced she wanted to take me down. I would never recommend working directly with a regulator. Ever! It is way smarter to hire an attorney, and in this case a securities attorney, and let them give you advice. The attorney you hire is on your side and can help you navigate the complexities of securities law. They can also communicate with the regulator on your behalf so you can stay compliant with the best possible outcome. Stay safe out there!

Cash

I understand this can be a controversial subject. This section simply shares my opinion on the advantages and disadvantages of using your own cash to buy a house.

I know a lot of investors pay cash for houses. It has become a very common way for investors to do deals. Here are some of the advantages to using this strategy.

Higher profits. Obviously, when you eliminate a loan, you save on lender fees and interest. That savings goes directly to the bottom line. For this reason, paying cash will produce the highest profits per deal of any financing option.

Comfort. Debt can be stressful, especially if you run into trouble and cannot make the payment. In 2008 and 2009, many real estate investors lost everything because they had loans. Leverage can be scary. When you pay cash, you will not have this stress, which can be a comfortable place to be.

More competitive. This is probably the biggest reason we are seeing so many cash transactions. Any advantage in getting deals is important. All else being equal, if you are paying cash and closing in a week and another investor is getting a loan, the seller is far more likely to take your offer. I know that some agents will instruct their clients to not consider any offer that is not all cash. This is especially true if there is major rehab needed.

How do you offer cash when you don't have any? It is possible to offer cash when using a loan, but you need to be careful with this. Lenders require title insurance, and most title insurance companies will not offer the correct policy if the contract restricts the use of loans. For this reason, if you do choose to offer cash, you need to give yourself the flexibility to use a loan in order to get the correct title insurance for your lender. Contracts can be different, but in most cases, there is an additional provisions section in which you can add custom agreement terms. Use this section if you offer all cash, and insert something similar to this: "Buyer reserves the right to fund this transaction with a loan as long as it does not affect the seller's net proceeds." Adding this language will allow the title company to issue the correct policy so you can get a loan if needed.

Although paying cash for a house has some clear advantages, I personally believe that the disadvantages of using your own cash to do deals outweigh the advantages. These are sometimes overlooked but are important to understand when making this decision. Here are some of the disadvantages to this strategy.

Target for lawsuits. I was driving my family home from Copper Mountain, a ski resort in Colorado, when I saw a billboard. "Hurt on the slopes?" the billboard started. "Give us a call," it continued. "We fight for you!" Basically, the message was if you got into a ski accident, you should call them so they could sue someone. These are what we call ambulance chasers. They run around looking for a reason to start a lawsuit. Most personal injury attorneys work on a contingency fee, meaning they charge their client a percent of the amount they are able to collect from the lawsuit. The key here is *a percent of the amount they collect*, not the amount they are awarded. Winning a lawsuit and collecting on it are two very different things. If you sue someone who is broke and cannot pay you, you will never get paid. The only way this is successful, outside of insurance companies, is to be sure the person they want to sue has assets that can be taken from them. You, as a real estate investor, will have assets that can be taken, so you will need to protect them.

Real estate is the most transparent asset there is. I can get online or look through one of the title company phone apps and tell you who owns a property and what loans are against it. Attorneys will do name searches, which are reports that disclose entities, assets, and liabilities for a particular person. When you own houses free and clear, it is public information. You can try to hide behind an LLC or other corporate structure, which is highly recommended, but that is not bulletproof, and attorneys can find assets through those. On the other hand, if the attorney does a search on you and all your properties appear to be leveraged, they may decide not to sue you in fear of not being able to collect.

Asset protection is a complicated subject and becomes more important as you grow your assets. The best defense is to not get sued in the first place, so the more broke you appear, the safer you are.

Lower return on investment. Some of the most important performance indicators for investors are their returns. How much money are they making on their money as a percentage? The formula is profits from your investment divided by the investment amount. So if you make $10,000 in a $100,000 investment, your return on investment is 10 percent. Because we know this formula works, we know that if we can reduce our investment, our return on that investment goes up. This is true even if we make a little less money on the deal.

Limiting. Obviously money is finite, unless you are the US government, I guess. When you pay cash for houses you limit the number of deals you can do. If your goal is to scale or do multiple deals, paying cash will restrict you. If you do decide to pay cash, I highly recommend that you keep at least enough money on the side for reserves and to meet any lender requirements to fund another deal just in case one falls into your lap. The last thing you want is to use all your money on one deal and have to pass on an even better deal.

More risk. Paying cash for houses carries a much higher degree of risk. Not only are you more likely to get targeted for lawsuits, but you are also putting a high amount of money into a deal. If that deal goes bad, there is no one to share the risk with. When you have a loan, you shift some risk to the lender. Now, you will likely have a personal guarantee, which is the lender's attempt to shift the risk of loss back to you, but the reality is by having a lender in tow, you can lean on them for help in troubling situations. Most lenders, especially hard-money lenders, would rather help you out of a jam than repossess a house.

Cash is king! If you have cash in the bank, you are protecting yourself. Reserves are important for any business, or family, for that matter. Having reserves gives you the flexibility to make mistakes and survive. If you have no reserves and you go over your budget, for example, you will not be able to finish the project. Money in the bank is also needed to get more loans. Lenders want to see you have liquidity, so keeping money in the bank keeps you bankable. If you have enough money to buy the house and keep a healthy reserve account, you will worry about this less, but do not pay all cash for a house if it drains your safety net.

Lines of Credit

Lines of credit come in many different forms. A line of credit is a creditor granting access to cash to be used when needed. Lines of credit usually allow you to draw on the account, use the money, pay it back, and then draw on it again. Some lines of credit, like credit cards, can go on indefinitely, while others, like commercial lines, will have draw periods and payback periods. What is fairly universal is the access to the cash when you need it and the responsibility to pay it back with interest. Here are the most common lines of credit used by real estate investors for fix-and-flips with some pros and cons for each.

Credit cards. I am not sure there needs to be much explanation here, but a credit card is a way to access a line of credit granted by a bank. You can use the credit card wherever the card is accepted to make purchases, and the credit card company will send in the money on your behalf. At the end of each month, they will send you a bill to pay them back. Any amount not paid back in that month will stay on the line as a balance and interest will be charged.

Although credit cards can get you into trouble there are some huge benefits that should not be overlooked. Credit cards are easy to get and provide a great way to access cash quickly. Many of them have perks, so by using them you can build up cash back or flyer miles. The big cards, like Master Card and Visa, are accepted almost everywhere, especially for materials, so credit cards are a fantastic way to purchase material for your project. It is also important to point out that you can borrow this money interest-free as long as you pay it back in full at the end of the month. Interest-free money with added perks…yes, I recommend that. It is my opinion that you should have a handful of credit cards for your real estate business, and I advise you to keep your business purchases on a separate card from your personal purchases. This makes it much easier to track, is easy to defend tax deductions if needed, and prevents you from commingling funds, which is a big no-no with most corporate structures.

As great as credit cards are, there are some downsides. The obvious one is that you can get yourself into real trouble with credit cards. They structure the minimum payment in a way that it is nearly impossible to pay the debt back if you make the minimum payment alone. Carrying a balance and then adding to that balance is a quick recipe for financial disaster. Although I believe you should have access to money, which is why I like credit cards, *do not* use them if you do not feel you can be responsible with them.

Credit cards are also very expensive if you do not pay them off every month. If you think hard money is expensive, I would not recommend looking at the rate your credit card company charges. They also have high late fees and possibly annual or monthly fees.

Credit card usage is also one of the fastest ways to ruin your credit report. An extremely high percentage of your credit score, I have heard as high as 30 percent, is based on credit usage. This is the balance on the card when it is reported compared to the credit limit. The higher it is, the harder it is on your credit score. It is true that your credit usage could affect your credit score more than late payments. As real estate investors, we need to be very protective of our credit. Business is so much easier when banks and lenders want to lend you money.

Supplier accounts. As you do more and more in this business, you will probably start opening up accounts with your preferred suppliers. Home Depot, for example, offers credit accounts to its customers, and so do many other suppliers. This works similarly to a credit card in that they will give you the material you need without a payment but will expect a payment within a set amount of time. This too is a great way to fund material costs as long as you can make the payment when due. This is very common when you are using hard money or some type of construction loan. When the payment on your account comes due, you can potentially request a draw on your loan to make the payment to your supplier. This keeps the project moving without waiting for a bank draw and without fronting the money from your pocket.

HELOC. I absolutely love HELOCs. A HELOC is a home equity line of credit. It is similar to a credit card in that you will have access to the cash whenever you need it, but the debt is secured by a home. Because the debt is secured, it offers extremely competitive interest rates and much larger line sizes. You will likely be giving access to the line through a checking account, so you can write checks or use a debit card to access the funds when you need it. I often see investors use HELOCs to purchase real estate or use the money as down payments on real estate.

One huge advantage to a HELOC is the line is secured by another property, so you will not need to go through a loan process to use it to buy more properties. If your line is large enough to buy a house in full, you can offer cash on the contract and close fast. These lines give you a great deal of flexibility.

They are getting harder to find on investment homes but are all over the place if you are willing to use your primary home as the collateral. I would start with your bank and ask what they offer and then shop around. Ask other investors where they got their line of credit and call those banks and credit unions too.

Business Line: Business lines of credit come in two primary forms, secured and unsecured. Most secured business lines are secured against accounts receivable or business equipment, neither of which real estate investors have much of. But if you have great credit, you can qualify for unsecured business lines to help with your investing. The problem with those is they are very expensive. Usually, you will have minimum usage limits, annual fees, and high rates. That means you may be paying for it even if you are not using it. If you think you will use it, they are probably worth exploring, but for most investors they are not worth the cost.

Pledged asset line. If you have investments in the stock market outside of your retirement account, you can likely establish a pledged asset line. These are lines of credit secured by the stock account. The line will have different advance rates based on the stability of the specific stock so you will have access from about 50 percent of the stock value up to a little over 90 percent. Why I love these is because you will have access to the money in your stock account without selling the stock. The risk with these are margin calls. If you lose value in your stock account, the lender may require that you pay down the line to stay within its advance rate. For this reason, I would never max out the line of credit unless you have the ability to come up with cash quickly in the event you lose value in your account. Most large brokerage firms will offer this but it may be called something different like a margin loan or line, flexible line, or loan management account.

Hard Money

Hard money is one of the most common ways fix-and-flip investors fund their deals. Unlike banks and the "banker speak," good hard-money lenders are reliable and understand your business. Hard-money lenders that have been in business for more than a decade, such as Pine Financial Group, got there because real estate investors can count on them. Ask around at your local real estate investment association or other investors who the best hard-money lenders are. If you are having trouble, Bigger Pockets has the largest and best directory of hard-money lenders. You can find that at: www.biggerpockets.com/real-estate-companies/hard-money-lenders.

Below is a simple example of how a fix-and-flip would look using hard money compared with how the deal would look if a bank loan were used.

Case Study: Niagara Street, Denver, Fix-and-Flip (Hard Money)

This property is located in Denver and was a fantastic find for our client. As the hard-money lender, were able to fund 100 percent of the purchase, repairs, and closing costs. Depending on your hard-money lender, when you are able to locate deals this strong, you might be able to borrow 100 percent of the costs. I am rounding these numbers for ease, but these are very close to the actual numbers on this deal.

After repaired value (ARV): $410,000

Purchase price: $222,000

Closing costs (to buy): $8,740

Repair budget: $55,000

Holding costs: $21,685 (loan payments, utilities, taxes, insurance)

Concessions: $2,500

Selling fees: $24,500

Profit = $75,575

You probably noticed right from the start that this was a fantastic deal. Purchasing a home that is potentially worth $410,000 for $222,000 leaves a lot of room. The investor found this deal because he was marketing for motivated sellers to call his company. This house was headed to foreclosure and needed a full remodel. The seller did not have enough time to sell the house any other way. The investor is one we have a relationship with, so when he called with the deal, we were ready. We funded it in about two weeks. This house is small, only 768 square feet with two bedrooms and one bathroom. As part of this investor's plan, the back door got moved slightly and the kitchen layout was altered for functionality. This plan created some much-needed living space.

Let's break down these numbers:

Closing cost to buy. The investor paid two points in origination. In this case, the total of points and other costs to close, which include title fees and government fees, was $8,740.

Repair budget: This was a smaller house, so the budget was not massive. He was able to complete the full rehab for about $55,000. That included opening up the layout, new bathroom, kitchen, paint, and floors.

Holding costs. Holding costs can be a tricky one for investors to calculate. It really comes down to accurately calculating the amount of time needed to rehab and sell the home. We will go into more detail about this when we learn the right way to analyze a fix-and-flip. In this example, the investor's total cost to hold this project was $21,685. Outside of taxes and insurance, this is actual cash out of the investor's pocket. I include taxes and insurance in the holding cost number because the amount you will pay in taxes and insurance is directly related to the amount of time you own the home. Taxes are paid "in arrears," which means that taxes for the current year are due in the following year. Insurance is prepaid, meaning you pay for it up front, but is included in the final settlement numbers and can potentially be included in the loan. Because insurance is paid up front, it is important for you as the property owner to remember to cancel that policy once you sell the house and get a refund for the unused premium. This, of course, assumes that any unused premium is, in fact, refundable.

Concessions. A concession is the seller giving the buyer something of value when they buy the house. It is like a bribe to buy the house. You as the seller can offer to pay a potential buyer's closing costs on their loan if they buy your house, for example. The most common concessions are credits toward the buyer's closing or loan costs, but they can be almost anything. Another common example is a seller credit for a repair or upgrade to the house. In this case study, the investor offered to credit the buyer $2,500 toward the buyer's closing costs.

Selling fees. The largest fee when selling a house is the real estate commission. These can vary and are negotiable. In this example, our client paid the listing agent five percent of the sale price, which covers both the buy-side commission and the commission to his listing agent. On top of this fee, you will need to pay title insurance premiums, title fees, and closing fees to the title company. In this example, all of the commission and closing fees were about $24,500.

When you run the numbers on a fix-and-flip, you always start with the end, the ARV, and then subtract all the costs to calculate the profit. Subtracting the purchase price, repairs, and other costs will give you the final profit. Here it was $75,575; not bad for one fix-and-flip on a 768-square-foot house!

From here, I would want to calculate the total return on investment or ROI. What was the investor's return on his money?

To calculate this, we need to figure out the total out-of-pocket costs and then divide his profit by his costs. Because Pine Financial Group, like many hard-money lenders, can loan up to 70 percent of the completed value, the total amount of the loan was $285,740. This is slightly under the maximum loan of 70 percent of ARV because this is all the buyer needed. Many hard-money lenders will loan up to 70 percent but will not loan more than the borrower needs to complete the project. Here, the loan amount was equal to the total amount he needed to close on the deal. If you add the purchase price of $222,000 to the repair costs of $55,000 and closing costs of $8,740 the result is $285,740. This was a true no-money-down deal for this client. The only out-of-pocket costs for this client were his holding costs, which we calculated to be $21,685. Remember, these included taxes and insurance. He did pay insurance before closing, but taxes were never out of his pocket. The total out-of-pocket cost was closer to $20,835.

Profit of $75,575 / out-of-pocket investment of $20,835 = 3.627

This is a 362.7 percent ROI.

If this deal took six months, which is close to what it did, the annualized return was closer to 725.4 percent. These are insane returns that are only possible when you can limit your out-of-pocket exposure as you can with hard money.

Now let's look at this exact same deal had the investor decided to go with a bank.

Case Study: Niagara Street, Denver (Bank Financing)

After repair value (ARV): $410,000

Purchase price: $222,000

Closing costs (to buy): $4,940

Repair budget: $55,000

Holding costs: $10,320 (loan payments, utilities, taxes, insurance)

Concessions: $2,500

Selling fees: $24,500

Profit = $90,740

Obviously, profits are higher because the amount of money borrowed to do the deal is lower. Borrowing less money saves on fees and interest. Most of the numbers are not affected by the financing you choose to use. The closing costs and holding costs are the two that will change. In this case, I used a bank loan amount of $193,900, which is equal to 70 percent of the purchase and repairs. This would assume a 30 percent equity requirement, which is very common for bank rehab loans.

Purchase of $222,000 + repairs of $55,000 = $277,000 × 70 percent = $193,900

I also assumed a one percent origination fee or one point to the lender, which is close to what you would expect. You can see closing costs come way down. For the holding cost number, I assumed a six percent bank rate and kept taxes, insurance, and utilities consistent. Had the investor chosen to use bank financing instead of hard money, he would have made $90,740 or an additional $15,165. Not too shabby!

Let's calculate the ROI. Because the bank would fund only 70 percent of his combined purchase and repairs, he would need to cover the other 30 percent. He would have also had to cover the closing costs and his holding costs. To stay consistent, I removed $850 from holding costs, which is approximately the tax payment that was never actually paid out of pocket. Total out-of-pocket holding costs in this example would have been $97,510. Total out-of-pocket investment is:

Bank down payment $83,100 + closing costs $4,940 + holding costs $9,470 = $97,510

Profit of $90,740 / out-of-pocket investment of $97,510 = .931

*That is a **93.1 percent** ROI*

Using bank financing would have given this investor a larger profit and still a fantastic return, but the return rate from using hard money was almost four times larger!

Hard money was the decision for this investor for more than just the higher return. Although he could have easily qualified for a bank loan, he chose hard money because he wanted to keep money in the bank. He prefers money in the bank so he can pounce on opportunities and keep a healthy reserve account. Using bank money will provide higher profits but will limit your ability to scale. If you are interested only in one deal at a time and want to maximize profits, bank debt is probably better. If you cannot qualify with the bank or you want to maximize what you can earn with the money you have available, you may want to consider hard money.

Chapter 3

BRRRR

How would you feel if you purchased rental property with 25 percent equity that had a cash flow of $500 or more per month, and you used none of your own money to do it? How many times would you repeat that?

True wealth is built by collecting assets that produce income. Fixing and flipping is a fantastic way to make a living, but it is a job. Once you stop flipping, your income stops. To win the game of wealth, investors focus on monthly passive cash flow.

Maybe you have heard it: "Local real estate investor builds massive portfolio of income producing properties." When I was getting started two decades ago, I heard this over and over again. It was in every real estate investment book, home study course, and late-night informational that I saw. It was usually the single mom becoming a multi-millionaire buying real estate as a side hustle. Although I knew it was true, there was always something missing in the real estate courses and books that I digested.

How exactly did they finance that many properties? How does the single mom afford that many down payments? The BRRRR method might be the best strategy that I have encountered in my 20 years and more than 2,500 deals. This is so powerful that using it will virtually guarantee your wealth.

The desired outcome of this strategy is to get into a property with as little money out of pocket as possible, while producing income and improving your balance sheet. You can do a heck of a lot more deals when you don't use much or any of your own money to purchase property. How many houses will it take to replace your current income?

THE STRATEGY

BRRRR stands for "buy, rehab, rent, refinance, repeat." There are a few different ways to accomplish this, but the best I have found involves a hard-money loan. You will also need a quality conventional lender and the ability to qualify for those conventional loans. Or you will need a partner able to qualify for conventional financing. Although "BRRRR" accounts for five steps, there are actually seven to make it successful: Locate the property, get it under contract and prepare a repair budget, get a hard-money acquisition loan, repair the property, rent the property, refinance the hard-money loan, and manage your investment.

Locate the Property

There are several keys to success here, but this is probably the most important piece to making this whole thing work, and probably the most challenging. As you will learn, the hard-money lender is going to limit the loan-to-value, so you need to find a deal with some serious upside that will also create cash flow. Usually, these deals are found in neighborhoods where you personally may not want to live. It is the lower income areas that have some depressed housing and maybe a higher percentage of vacancies and foreclosures, the neighborhoods that have a higher percentage of renters to owners. These are the areas that tend to produce the highest cash flow, which creates the opportunity for successful use of this strategy.

Most of the deals are still found in the MLS with the help of a Realtor, but there are a number of ways to find deals. We have already discussed some strategies to locate deals, such as direct marketing, cold calling, knocking on doors, and signs. Because locating the property is beyond the scope of this book, I would encourage you start by meeting with a local agent who has experience finding these types of deals. You can also get ideas on located deals with little to no marketing budget on our YouTube channel:

www.youtube.com/pinefinancial

Get It Under Contract and Prepare a Repair Budget

Now it's time to put the deal together. I recommend getting the contract in place before you put together a detailed budget. I don't mean go out there and make 200 blind offers with no idea of value and waste your Realtor's time, but don't do all your diligence and spend time putting together a full repair budget when you don't know if you have a deal. I recommend making offers based on a good guesstimate of value and a healthy repair budget. Ideally, you want the purchase price plus repairs and closing costs to be equal to or less than 70 percent of the value because this is the maximum loan of many hard-money lenders.

The point here is to make offers that you are confident you will close on, and make those offers before you have too much time into the deal and remember the 70 percent rule. If you cannot be all in for under 70 percent, get as close as you can to limit your out of pocket.

Once you have the contract, spend the time running all the numbers and be sure that your contractor gives you a solid estimate of what it will cost to repair. I normally recommend walking the project and completing a spreadsheet with the work you want done. Give that spreadsheet to multiple contractors so they are all bidding on the same work. Be sure to budget for contingencies because there are repairs that you don't see. Once all your analysis is done, you will then decide whether to move forward and close on the deal or kill it because the numbers don't work.

If you decide to move forward, you will need an estimate of repairs broken down, so that it is clear what will be done to the property. Successful investors live and die by the budgets, and this is essential for the hard-money lender to come up with the value and determine their interest in your deal. You can download the spreadsheet we use for this at www.fundyourflip.com The spreadsheet you are looking for is called Scope of Work.

Get Hard-Money Acquisition Loan

Once you have the contract and the repair budget put together, you can run the deal by your hard-money lender. As long as the total cost to do the deal is at or below 70 percent of the value, many hard-money lenders will loan you 100 percent of your costs, making this a no-money-down loan. When running numbers, I would use the term "acquisition costs" to include the purchase price, the repairs, and all the closing costs to buy the property. It can be tricky to determine the closing costs, so call your lender and make sure you understand *all* their fees and any other fees that will be included in the closing. We go through these numbers in detail later in the book.

Here's an example of what you can pay and keep a deal no-money-down with this strategy. Let's say you find a house in a neighborhood that rents well, and the house would sell for $150,000 if you decided to sell it. You know that it is going to take you $12,000 to get the house ready to rent. This will include new carpet and paint, used appliances, kitchen and bath refresh, and some other minor repairs. Since the value is $150,000, your HML will loan you $105,000. ($150,000 × 70 percent)

$105,000 (start with the loan amount)

−$12,000 (repairs)

−$4,100 (estimated total closing costs)

−$88,900 (maximum offer for a zero-down deal)

Again, don't get too hung up on these numbers yet. We will go through these in detail later since the numbers are an extremely important piece of your investment success. For now, understand that for this strategy to work, you will want a hard-money loan in place for the purchase and repair of the house.

Repair Property

Once you close on the house, you will want your contractor to complete the repairs as soon as possible. Your hard-money lender will issue repair funds to you on a draw schedule as the work is completed. It is important for you to understand how the draw process works and structure a schedule with your contractor that you can accomplish. Many times, I see real estate investors get into trouble because they are promising their contractor money before the hard-money lender is able to release it. There should be a very clear process on how the draws work.

Managing the project and your contractor is beyond what we can cover in this book, but I will make a few important points.

It is extremely important to have a contract with your contractor. In this agreement, you will spell out the terms of the payments and the timeline. This is what you will use to hold your contractor accountable.

You should consider getting lien waivers for any payments that you make to them. If there is ever a conflict with your contractor, the first thing they will do is file a lien, which can make it very difficult to refinance the hard-money loan. A lien waiver is an acknowledgment by them that they have been paid and it waives their rights to lien your property.

Make your selections early. If the contractor does not have clear instructions, they will leave the job site and go to another job. This will slow you way down. And trust me, you don't want them making design decisions.

Keep good records of everything you can. There are many reasons for this, but it could come in handy if you have any trouble with the appraisal for your refinance. The appraiser will need to understand why the house is worth so much more than you paid for it. Showing the work that was completed will help.

Rent the Property

As you are finishing the repairs, get your "For Rent" sign in the yard. People who go by and see that you are rehabbing a house will be interested. They will be even more interested if they know that it will be for rent. Don't put the sign out while the house is torn apart. Wait until it is coming together so the average person can see how nice it will be. There is something very attractive about being the first to live in a freshly remodeled home, so this is when demand for your home will be the highest.

Although you cannot get the loan until the house is complete and the appraiser can walk through a freshly remodeled home, you can certainly start the loan process. It is best to start that process as soon as you have a signed lease, so getting one quickly can save you big!

Refinance Hard-Money Loan

Here is the beauty and part of the magic that makes this happen. At the time of writing this book, Fannie Mae will allow you to do a rate and term refinance on a house with no title seasoning. This means that as long as you are paying off a current loan and not taking cash out, they don't care how long you have owned the home. They will use the new appraised value. The Fannie Mae loan can be obtained through any good mortgage company. If you are working in an area that we work in, we have great lenders who can help with this. Please see our referral page on our website if you need to find a lender who understands this strategy and can help get this refinance done: https://pinefinancialgroup.com/about-us/we-recommend/.

For a single-family home, the refinance loan will allow you to borrow up to 75 percent of the new appraised value. Remember that the hard-money lender only loaned you 70 percent, so you can roll all your closing costs into the new loan and have no out-of-pocket expenses with the refinance. In this scenario, the only money required is the money to make the payments on the loans, and you might not even need that. If you are fast, you can get the property rehabbed and a tenant in place producing income before you make your first payment.

Timing your closing is a skillful strategy used by the best real estate investors. Most hard-money lenders will collect interest payments in arrears, due the month after the loan is out. If the hard-money lender wants all their payments due on the first of the month, they will prorate the first month's interest payment and then collect the second month in arrears, so you will skip the first month's payment. This is important to understand because you can time your closing for maximum benefit. If your lender operates like this, then your strategy could be to close as early in the month as possible and pay that first month's interest at closing. If there is enough room in the deal, your hard-money lender may allow you to roll that interest payment into the closing costs and into the loan. You would then skip a month's payment, essentially giving you two months with no payment. Depending on the level of rehab, you just might be able to get a tenant to pay enough in rent to cover those payments before your first one is due and while you complete your refinance. Your refinance lender will act in the same manner. They will most likely allow you to roll the first interest payment into the loan and they too will skip a month to be sure the loan payments are made in arrears. Assuming you can close on the purchase early in the month and get your refi done in two months, it is possible to go almost four months without making a payment.

Some lenders cannot use the new appraised value for this refinance. They will require that you own the property for a set amount of time before they can refinance you or they will use your purchase price as the value. This hold time could be six to twelve months. If you hear this, understand that this is a lender overlay. Lender overlays are common in real estate finance. An overlay is simply a guideline put in place by that specific lender. These are guidelines on top of the conventional underwriting guidelines. Lenders will sometimes use overlays to be more conservative to help ensure that Fannie Mae or Freddie Mac will purchase the loans. Because these guidelines are specific to lenders, they vary among lenders. If you are trying to implement this strategy and the lender tells you that you need to own the home for six to twelve months, understand that this is an overlay and that you should call a different lender.

One potential pitfall of this strategy is the appraisal for your refinance. Because an appraiser gives only one person's opinion of the value, appraised values can vary among appraisers. If the appraiser for your refinance believes the home is worth less than the appraiser for your purchase did, your lender may not loan you enough to accomplish your goal. This is a potential problem you should get in front of. The good news is that for your refinance, you will already own the home, so the appraiser needs to contact you for access. This gives you an advantage. When they call you, schedule a time to meet them there. Never give them the lock box and allow them access without you. In that meeting, you can discuss your strategy and how you improved the property, maybe show some before and after pictures. I would also search for recent comps that would support your value, and I would absolutely share the appraisal from your purchase. Anything you can do to make their job easier and show that you have done your homework will help them understand why the property is worth so much more than you paid for it. I have also heard from multiple lenders that ordering the appraisal on a rush and paying the rush fee is worth it because those tend to come in where you expect them to, especially if you are providing them with the comps they can use. I doubt an appraiser would ever admit to this, but I have been told this is an effective strategy multiple times.

Manage Your Investment

This is pretty self-explanatory. Once you have a cash cow for a rental property, you need to be sure it is managed. Managing property yourself is not that hard, and I highly recommend it to any new investor before you consider hiring property management. How do you know if the management company is doing a good job if you don't know what it takes to manage property?

I still manage most of my own properties. I do have a handful of out-of-state rentals that I have hired management for. These are small deals, and sometimes my attention is not focused on them. There have been times when they have sat vacant for extended periods of time or work orders have not been completed in a timely manner. I have also had tenants move out because they could not get along with the manager. Right now, I am working on moving these to another new manager, my third, to see if I can improve performance. I also recently moved five condos I own in the Denver area over to a local manager because I was sick of dealing with the HOAs. I was not getting any support dealing with issues that needed multiple units to work together. The day I had to drive out there and start knocking on doors was the day I decided to hire a manager. Since then, I have found that I am working just as hard to keep these properties operating at a high level. I believe I would be at a big-time disadvantage if I did not already have some property management experience.

Repeat

On to the next one. Do the entire process over and over and build a million-dollar cash flowing portfolio.

CASE STUDIES

These are actual deals in which we have participated. The first one is a perfect example of what we see several times a month and one that you should be able to find. The second example is one of those home runs you don't see every day. Remember that actual results may vary. I wanted to include both so that you get an idea of what to expect and what is also possible if you are putting in the effort. You can't find deals like these if you don't look.

Deal 1: Minneapolis

Our client purchased this home for $105,000 in Minneapolis, Minnesota, and repaired it for approximately $50,000. This included a new driveway, exterior siding, and a full cosmetic remodel of the interior. The property is a little under 2,000 square feet with the basement and contains four bedrooms and two bathrooms. The closing costs were $6,525, making the total acquisition $161,525. I consider the acquisition costs a combination of all three of the purchase, repairs, and closing costs. I do this because with a repair escrow account, you need to fund all three of these at the time you close on the purchase. The after repaired appraisal for the hard money was $245,000. He had a whopping $100 in earnest money, which he got back at closing, making this a true no-money-down deal. He then refinanced the home with a new loan of $165,000 and was able to roll the refinance costs into the new loan. He has it rented for $1,500, and his monthly payment after the refinance with taxes and insurance is $1,218. Here is how it looks:

- *Purchase: $105,000*
- *Repairs: $50,000*
- *CC: $6,525*
- *Acquisition: $161,525*
- *Value: $245,000*
- *Hard-money loan: $161,525*
- *Money to closing: $0*
- *Refinance cost: $3,400*
- *Refinance loan: $165,000*
- *PITI: $1,218 (This was a six percent interest rate and a thirty-year loan)*
- *Rent $1,500*
- *Gross cash flow: $282*

Because this was such a large rehab, it took him about five months to complete the work and find a tenant. During that time, he had $8,682 in hard-money loan interest payments. If we combine the payments with the cash to close, we get $8,682 ($0 + $8,682). That makes this investment a **39.0 percent** return on investment ($282 cash flow × 12 months/$8,682 money in deal). This does not even include the equity in the property, which is another **$80,000,** tax benefits, or the fact that the tenant is paying off his loan. Taking out the $80,000 in instant equity, his total first year return is actually closer to **203.4 percent.**

$3,384 in positive cash flow

$2,026 in principal reduction

$12,250 in appreciation (this is based on a five percent appreciation rate which is below average but is not guaranteed)

$17,660 total profit in first year divided by the investment of $8,682 is **203.4 percent!**

Where else are you getting this kind of return?

Deal 2: Pueblo

This is the home run deal that we don't see every day. I wanted to include it because this is the type of deal that is possible. Our client purchased this home for $150,000. It is a triplex in an old neighborhood in southern Colorado. It is a lower income area, so our client did a pretty basic remodel to get it ready to rent. The total budget for his repairs was $65,000. This included paint and carpet, new exterior with windows, updated kitchens with floors, counters, and painted cabinets, and some bathroom cleanup. His closing costs ended up being about $7,550, and the building appraised for $325,000. His total acquisition was $222,550, and based on the value of $325,000, we loaned him $222,550. This covered all his costs, making it a no-money-down loan. It cost him another $4,300 in refinance costs with a new refinance loan of $226,850. He was able to roll all the refinance costs into the new loan. Because it is a multifamily building, he is able to get more in rent. This little tri-plex is currently rented for $2,900 per month, and the payment on his new loan with taxes and insurance is $1,435. That is a gross monthly cash flow of **$1,465** every month before vacancies and maintenance. He did have to make two hard-money loan payments totaling $4,785. Here is how the deal turned out:

- *Purchase: $150,000*
- *Repairs: $65,000*
- *CC: $7,550*
- *Acquisition: $222,550*
- *Value: $325,000*
- *Hard-money loan: $222,550*
- *Money to closing: $0*
- *Refinance cost: $4,300*
- *Refinance loan: $226,850*
- *PITI: $1,435*
- *Rent $2,900*
- *Gross cash flow: $1,465*

To calculate his total cash on cash return, I take the annual cash flow $1,465 × 12 months = $17,580, and I divide that by his investment, which is two hard-money loan payments for a total of $4,785. Calculating the total return $17,580/$4,785 = **367.4 percent** return on investment. This does not include the $98,150 in instant equity or any of the other benefits such as appreciation, principal reduction, or tax benefits!

Deal 3: Denver

I thought it would be interesting to see what would have happened if our client had decided to keep the project on Niagara. Niagara was the first case study we went over. Our client flipped it and made more than $75,000, but what if he kept it?

Purchase: $222,000

Repairs: $45,000 (I reduced this by $10,000 because our strategy is to refinance and rent. In that case, we will not do as nice of a job with our rehab. We would likely use used appliances for example)

CC: $8,460 (this number changed a little because our loan amount is a tad less. The difference is negligible, however)

Acquisition: $275,460 (this is the total of purchase price, repairs, and closing costs)

Value: $390,000 (I reduced this $20,000 to be conservative, but also if we are doing less work to improve the house, it is possible that the house would be worth less)

Hard-money loan: $273,000 (70 percent of the estimated ARV)

Money to closing: $2,460

Refinance cost: $4,900 (this includes origination, title fees, and the new appraisal)

Refinance loan: $277,900 (you can see that we would be able to roll the full amount of the refinance costs into the loan so the only money into this deal was the original $2,460 he would have had to bring to closing plus any payment he would have made on the hard-money loan)

PITI: $1,916 (I used a six percent interest rate and $250 for taxes and insurance)

Rent $2,200 (this is estimated based on rent comps)

Gross cash flow: $284

If it took four months to complete the rehab and refinance, we would have four hard-money loan payments for an additional $11,739 out of pocket. Total out of pocket with the $2,460 required when the property was purchased and the four payments total $14,199.

To calculate his total cash on cash return, I take the annual cash flow $284 × 12 months = $3,408, and I divide that by his investment, which is $14,199 ($3,408 / $14,199) = **24.0 percent** return on investment. Not a home run by any stretch, but it would have created a 24 percent return in year one plus room for rent growth, paying down the loan, appreciation, tax benefits, and the fact that there is already equity in the property.

If he can reduce the time to rehab the house and it only took three months, the total payments would have been $8,804 plus the $2,460 down for a total out of pocket of $11,264. In this case the return would shoot up to **30.3 percent,** year after year after year. His $75,000 in profit would still be there as equity in the home, and he would have created an income stream he can count on. This is how true wealth is created!

RUNNING THE NUMBERS

There are two primary ways to run your numbers on a new potential purchase when you plan to use the BRRRR strategy. You can come up with a price and back into a return like we did on all the case studies, or you can look at required cash flow and down payment and come up with a maximum amount you are able to pay. Since we have already reviewed how to calculate returns based on current numbers, I wanted to focus this section on coming up with a price you can pay for a target property. This is how you come up with your offer and the maximum amount you can pay for a property.

The first step is to determine the maximum loan amount that can be placed on the property. To calculate this, we start with the NOI, or net operating income, then subtract our required cash flow. The Maximum Loan Worksheet can be found in the appendix. Here is how the formula looks. Monthly rent vacancy – Maintenance – Taxes and insurance – Other expenses = NOI. We then subtract out required cash flow. NOI – Required cash flow = Maximum principal and interest payment. Finally, we use the monthly mortgage payment to find the maximum loan. We built a calculator to do this for you which you can have for free on at www.fundyourflip.com.

We always start with gross potential rent, which is the monthly expected rent you will be able to collect. Then subtract a vacancy factor to account for the vacancies. A five percent vacancy factor is the most common, but you can research actual vacancy rates in your area.

Maintenance can be all over the place and is by far the hardest factor to predict. For single-family homes, this is normally lower than you would see with multifamily buildings with common areas, but one furnace or water heater will change things in a hurry. For a standard rental, I would use somewhere between 10 percent and 15 percent of the monthly rent as a budget for maintenance. This will include a reserve to replace for larger items like a water heater or furnace so similar to a vacancy factor, you won't be spending this each month, but this will get you close to an average cost over a period of time and should be accounted for in your numbers.

Taxes will come from the county and possibly, a city as well. I learned this one the hard way. I own several single-family homes in Memphis, Tennessee, and accounted for the taxes the county would be collecting when I ran my numbers. What I did not know was that the city also charged property taxes and the first year I was surprised to learn that I owed additional taxes. These are small rentals, and that additional tax bill wiped out nearly a full month of rent I collected and drastically changed my returns. I also received a bill from the state for income taxes for the income I generated in the state. Be sure you are aware of all municipalities that will be charging taxes for owning property.

The insurance premium will come from your agent.

Other expenses would include utilities that you as the owner plan to pay, administration costs, and management fees. I did not include any management fee, but it might be a good idea to do so. A good rule of thumb for management is eight percent to 10 percent of the gross rent.

Your NOI is calculated by subtracting the vacancy factor and all the expenses from the gross rent. For commercial property, you would expect to analyze your NOI on an annual basis. For residential, it is much easier to keep all the numbers on a monthly basis.

From here, I subtract the minimum cash flow I would be willing to accept. This gives me my maximum principal and interest payment. To get a maximum loan from this number, you need a very specific calculator or to be a whiz with excel. Because this can be tricky we created the calculator for you which is available at: www.fundyourflip.com.

If you were making a traditional purchase with a 25 percent down payment, you would simply divide the maximum loan by 75 percent (or whatever the total LTV ratio is for the lender) and subtract estimated closing costs to come up with your maximum offer. With the BRRRR strategy, though, we need to take a second step.

The maximum loan that we calculate is the final loan. To come up with the maximum hard-money loan for our acquisition, we need to deduct an estimate for the cost to close the refinance. The best way to do this is to call your lender, but if you wanted to try to calculate this yourself, you can. Most conventional lenders will charge a one percent origination fee and there will be about one percent more in additional fees which will include the appraisal. Since we know it will be about two percent total in fees, we can take the maximum loan and multiply that by 98 percent. This will give us the maximum hard-money loan for our acquisition.

Once we have the maximum hard-money loan, we can add any money we are willing to use as down payment to come up with our maximum acquisition costs. If we subtract our cost of repairs and the closing costs to buy from the acquisition cost, we will end up with our maximum offer price. I know this is all a little tricky because of the multiple moving parts, but stick with me and we will go through an example to help you better understand the numbers.

The final step is to ensure that the maximum acquisition loan (the hard-money loan that we plan to use for the purchase) is less than or equal to the hard-money lender's LTV guidelines. If it is, then we are good to make the offer. If not, we would need to further reduce the offer to hit the hard-money lender's guidelines.

I know this gets extremely complicated, but all of this is important. Numbers are part of the business, so let's go through a hypothetical example.

EXAMPLE

Let's say we find a house in an area we know well and that all the three bed, two bath homes sell for $200,000 once they are fixed up. We also know that the rent for this $200,000 home is $1,600 per month. We really like the area, so we are always looking at the homes that hit the market and see one that is recently available through the MLS. After viewing the home, we see it needs some work and estimate this to cost us about $30,000. Finally, we won't consider a deal that makes us less than $200 in monthly cash flow. What do we offer?

$1,600 Monthly rent
−$80 Vacancy (5 percent)
−$160 Maintenance (10 percent)
−$250 Taxes & insurance
= $1,110 NOI
−$200 Required cash flow
= $910 Max principal & interest

$151,780 Max loan amount (I used a six percent interest rate and a 30-year loan with the calculator I found online)
X 98 percent

$148,744 Max hard-money loan

−$30,000 repairs
−$5,475 closing costs (we will go into more detail on this in a later section)
= **$113,269** Offer price

This assumes a no-money-down deal. If you are willing to put some money into the deal, you can add that to this number to increase your offer. This also considers that the tenant pays utilities and that there is no property manager.

To verify that we are under the hard-money lender's guidelines and can borrow this amount of money, we need to multiply the ARV of $200,000 by 70 percent (or whatever the hard-money lender's LTV guideline is).

$200,000 × 70 percent = $140,000

Because the maximum hard-money acquisition loan in our analysis is *more* than the maximum amount the hard-money lender will lend us using the 70 percent rule, we would need to lower our offer by the difference. In this case, the offer would need to come down by $8,744 ($148,744: $140,000). The total maximum offer is **$104,525**.

I want to stress that this is for a no-money-down deal. You can always increase your offer price any amount that you would be willing to apply to the purchase.

It might be a good idea to run these numbers on several deals to get the hang of it. Go back through this section with deals you want to make offers on and practice running your numbers. Again the calculator available for free at www.fundyourflip.com is a great fast and easy way to run these numbers.

BRRRR RISKS

Although BRRRR is one of the most powerful strategies used to build million-dollar portfolios, it does not come without risks. Here are some of the primary risks to be aware of and strategies to limit those risks.

Construction

This is a risk whether you are implementing the BRRRR strategy, fixing and flipping, or just turning over a rental. Construction costs are on the rise, and staying within a budget can be challenging. Even the most successful investors go over their budget and over the expected time to complete the project. If you are using the BRRRR strategy and counting on rental income to make the hard-money loan payments, you could find yourself in trouble if you are not able to get the property rehabbed in time. It is probably a good idea to include a contingency in your budget and have some reserves on the sideline for payments until you can get your rehab complete and rented.

Appraisal Risk

The risk here is if the appraisal for your refinance comes in lower than you expected. If that does happen, your refinance loan amount will be reduced, and you will be required to bring cash to closing. If you don't have the cash needed, you will be forced to pay off the hard-money loan without the refinance, which usually means selling the property. Remember, the refinance lender will loan up to 75 percent of the value and you likely borrowed at 70 percent of the value, so there is a small five percent buffer. We discussed some tips to lessen this risk earlier in this section.

No Longer Qualify

There is always the chance that you will not qualify for the refinance loan. This is why I strongly recommend that you prequalify for the refinance before you buy the house. That is not bulletproof, however. It is also possible that your situation changes or the guidelines change before you close on that refinance. Investors do some funny things, like buy a car and take on new debt, for example, before they get their refinance done. If your strategy is to refinance your hard-money loan, you might want to avoid anything that could impact your qualification. If this does occur, I have seen investors bring in partners who qualify for the loan for a piece of the deal. It is much better to share a deal than lose a deal.

Rent Lower Than Expected

Before you buy the house, you will run your numbers to ensure you will be getting the return you are expecting. I recently purchased a one-bedroom condo in Denver, and believed that I could get $1,200 per month in rent. This was a pretty simple deal with a decent expected return, but it was no home run. I had my leasing agent all lined up, and he agreed with my numbers. He started marketing the property about a week before my completion date and all we heard were crickets. Four weeks later, I called him, and he said he is not getting responses to the ads that he would expect and had only walked one potential tenant through the unit. I knew we were wrong on our rent estimate, and I know that price fixes everything. We ended up renting the unit for $1,050, and it took two months to do it. It has gone up in value and still has cash flow, but barely.

I research rent rates online. Sometimes you can find these in the MLS or online rent advertisements, and your leasing agent should have an idea too. You can also use rent estimators like Zillow or rent-o-meter.com. All of that works, but the best way to find the rent amount is to knock on some doors in the neighborhood, tell them you like the area and are considering renting a home, and then ask how much other people pay in rent. You will be surprised. If they rent, they will tell you what they pay, and if they don't rent, they normally know what their neighbors are paying. You might also consider adding in a small buffer to your numbers. If you really need only $200 a month in cash flow, you might run the numbers at $300 just in case your rent estimate is off.

Interest Rate Risk

Interest rates will also affect your cash flow. If rates increase during the time between your purchase and your refinance, your mortgage payment will be higher than you expected. You can mitigate this risk by getting your rehab done quickly and locking in an interest rate with your lender as soon as you can. Work with your lender and discuss options on when to lock your rate.

When you can leverage into property with little or no money down, your returns go through the roof. Other than real estate, what investment will return more 200 percent year after year like we saw with our real-life case studies? You will also increase your ability to build a portfolio. The less cash you put into each deal, the more deals you can do.

Chapter 4

Fix-and-Flip Investor Formulas

There are just a handful of important formulas to understand as a fix-and-flip investor. These formulas are more specific to using a hard-money lending as your funding source but will work no matter how you fund your deal.

QUICKLY ANALYZE THE DEAL

Purchase + Repairs / ARV

If you were to call your lender about a deal you are looking at, they are going to want to know three numbers: the price you are paying, the amount of your rehab, and the value once completed. From that, they will use this formula. When you combine the purchase and repairs and divide by the value, you will get a percentage for an answer:

> < 70% = good deal
>
> > 70% & < 75% = should profit
>
> > 75% & < 80% = probably too tight but might work
>
> > 80% = Punt

If that percentage is less than 70 percent, you have a good deal. If it is between 70 percent and 75 percent, you probably have a good deal, and it is worth looking into further. If it is 75 percent to 80 percent, your deal is starting to get tight and is probably too risky to pursue. Anything over 80 percent is a hard pass! Do not even consider deals this high, especially if you are using hard money. Obviously, we are leaving closing costs out of this formula, but this is just a nice and easy way to quickly look at potential deals.

MAXIMUM LOAN

ARV × 70 Percent

This will depend on the hard-money lender's maximum loan-to-value and loan-to-cost ratios. For us, it is simple because we don't have a loan-to-cost ratio and we loan 70 percent of the ARV. Many hard-money lenders will loan a percent of cost not to exceed a percent of the value. For example, they may loan you 90 percent of purchase and 90 percent of repairs up to 60 percent of value. In these cases, you would need to calculate the maximum loan based on your cost and value and use the lesser of the two.

MONTHLY PAYMENT

Loan Amount × Interest Rate / 12

As discussed, almost every hard-money lender will use simple interest to come up with a monthly payment. The formula is to calculate the annual payment and divide by 12.

MAO

This is your maximum allowable offer. The amount you can pay for the property and be profitable. There are two different ways we run our numbers to determine what we should be paying for a fix-and-flip. The first and easiest is the Max Loan Method. This is well known in the industry as the 70 percent rule. The second method is the Profit Method. The Max Offer Worksheet with both methods is in the appendix of the book. You can also download free copies at www.fundyourflip.com

Max Loan Method

To use the Max Loan Method, we work through a three-step process.

1. Calculate the maximum loan you can get.

2. Calculate the closing costs.

3. Back into your offer.

The complete formula is below. The maximum loan is 70 percent of the ARV, and the closing costs represent two points in origination plus some additional title fees. We are using 70 percent maximum LTV and two points, but you would adjust these numbers to match your hard-money lender's expectations on LTV and pricing. For the worksheet, we used $2,500 for the additional fees. This covers title fees, recording fees, closing fees, and any other fees that would be associated with your closing. I used $2,500 because I believe it to be very close to what you will see in most markets, but it could be more or less depending on the title fees and the size of your deal.

It would be easiest to understand if you view the worksheet in the appendix or download it from the website as we work through the formula. The Max Loan Method starts with calculating the maximum you can borrow. For most hard-money lenders, you can borrow 70 percent, so we start by taking the ARV and multiplying that by 70 percent to get our maximum loan. If the hard-money lender will loan more or less than 70 percent, you will want to use their guideline here. After that we need to calculate our closing costs to purchase the home. You do this by multiplying the maximum loan by the lender points and then add in the flat fee and title fees. In our example we are using two points and $2,500 in flat lender and title fees. As mentioned, it has been my experience that $2,500 in flat lender and title fees covers about everything. If the lender has high administration fees or the title company charges more than what I am used to, this could be higher. The final number you will need is the repair budget. Calculating that is outside the scope of this book but there are tons of great books and resources on the best way to come up with the repair budget. For me, I go through the house and look at everything I would like to do and put it in a spreadsheet. I then have multiple contractors bid based on that spreadsheet. This way we are comparing apples to apples. Every contractor will have their own ideas on what needs to be done so I would include those as a separate section of the spreadsheet or a different one altogether. Listen to what they say because they will likely give you some great advice. Over time and reviewing contractor bids you will easily be able to create these budgets on your own.

Once you have the maximum loan, the closing costs, and the repair estimate you are ready to calculate your maximum offer. Start with the Maximum Loan and subtract both the repair budget and closing costs. This is your maximum offer if you are looking for a true no-money-down deal.

Loan: __$300,000__ × __70%__ = __$210,000__
     ARV

Closing Costs: __$210,000__ × __2%__ + __$2,500__ = __$6,700__
     Max Loan

Offer Price: __$210,000__ Max Loan

− __$50,000__ Repairs

− __$6,700__ Closing Costs

= __$153,300__ **Max Offer**

Let's use a hypothetical example. Let's use a $300,000 ARV house that needs $50,000 in repairs. We calculate the loan amount by taking $300,000 and multiplying it by 70 percent to get a maximum loan amount of $210,000. We follow that by calculating our closing costs by taking the maximum loan amount of $210,000, multiplying it by two percent and then adding $2,500 to get $6,700. Finally, we came up with our maximum offer by starting with our maximum loan of $210,000 and then subtracting $50,000 for the repairs and $6,700 for the closing costs giving us an offer amount of $153,300.

Profit Method

Often, after we go through this formula, I get pushback. "What about the taxes?" "What about your holding costs?" "What about [fill in the blank]?" I am glad you asked! Let's go through our second method of analyzing a deal.

The idea here is to come up with a maximum offer based on the amount of money you want to make. The formula for your MAO using the Profit Method is: ARV minus the profit you want to make minus all your expenses. These include; closing costs when you buy, repairs you plan to make, all your holding costs, any expected concessions, Realtor fees, and closing costs when you sell.

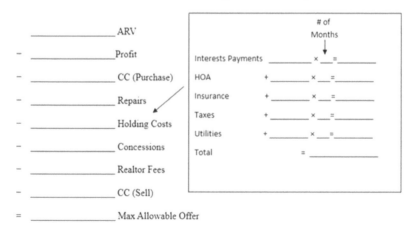

Notice that list price is not in this formula anywhere. We do not use list price or asking price in any way when coming up with an offer. We can use list price as a data point for finding deals, but that is it. The bottom line is we don't care what the seller wants for their house. I am told all the time that an investor got a great deal because he or she was able to negotiate a big discount from the asking price. My first thought is always, "Maybe they were overpriced to begin with and you just negotiated to pay full price." We need to offer based on what the property can afford for us to pay. Period.

If we were to use the same hypothetical example of a $300,000 ARV and $50,000 in repairs the worksheet would look like this:

$300,000 ARV minus $50,000 profit minus $6,700 closing costs to purchase minus $50,000 repairs minus $13,625 holding costs minus $2,500 concessions minus $18,000 Realtor fees minus $3,000 closing costs to sell, which equals $156,175 as our Max Allowable Offer.

	$300,000	ARV
−	$50,000	Profit
−	$6,700	CC (Purchase)
−	$50,000	Repairs
−		Holding Costs

Again, we start with the end value and then subtract our profits first. Most "experts" teach you to run your numbers as we did with our case studies. Start with the end value and subtract all the costs to end up with your profit. I believe it is much smarter to pay yourself first and come up with a maximum price you can pay based on the minimum profits you are willing to accept.

After determining the amount we are comfortable making, we calculated the closing costs to purchase which was done in the Max Loan Method so we use that number as our closing costs here.

The repair budget was also used in the Max Loan Method. This is the total amount needed to make all the repairs to the property.

Now we need to calculate the holding costs. Holding costs can be a bit tricky, so I broke that out in a separate box on our worksheet in the appendix. The first step to completing this is to estimate the total amount of time you will own the property. The three stages to consider are the time it will take to rehab the house, the time needed to market the home and find a buyer, and the time to close the transaction. For this example, I am going to assume it will take us about three months to rehab the house because it is a significant $50,000 remodel. We are in a decent market as I write this, so I will use one month for marketing time and one additional month to close the transaction. If my assumptions are accurate, we will own this house for a total of five months. This means that each monthly expense will need to be multiplied by five to calculate the total holding costs. To start, I put a five in the blank line after each monthly expense to be sure I multiple each item by the amount of time I will own the home. Now it's just going line by line down the list.

	# of Months	
Interests Payments	_____ × 5 =	_____
HOA	+ _____ × 5 =	_____
Insurance	+ _____ × 5 =	_____
Taxes	+ _____ × 5 =	_____
Utilities	+ _____ × 5 =	_____
Total	=	_____

Interest payments. Our monthly interest payment on the hard-money loan will be our largest expense. All hard-money lenders I know charge interest on a simple interest basis. This means they do not amortize the loan, so you will be paying interest only each month and no principal. This makes it simple to calculate. This formula was covered earlier in the chapter. You start with your loan amount and multiply it by your interest rate. That gives you the annual interest payment. If you divide that by 12, you will end up with your monthly payment. For this example the loan amount is $210,000 and the interest rate is 12 percent. In that case, I would multiply $210,000 by 12 percent to get my annual interest of $25,200. Divide by 12 and my monthly interest payment is $2,100: $210,000 × 12 percent / 12 = $2,100.

HOA. HOA is a homeowner's association. This association can play many different roles, and each HOA is a little different. Some examples of HOA responsibilities are: covenant enforcement, trash or other utilities, amenities such as parks, pools, or a clubhouse, and common area maintenance. In this example, the house is not in an HOA, so we have $0 expense with this. As a side note, some HOAs have transfer fees, so be sure to keep an eye out for that and work that into your numbers.

Insurance. Insurance is the property insurance. This premium is usually paid in advance at closing. There are a few points I want to make about insurance.

- Many insurance agents do not understand the fix-and-flip business. When you call and ask for insurance, they will likely ask you if you plan to live in the home. Your answer of course is no, in which case they provide you a landlord policy instead of a primary home policy. The problem with a landlord policy is they all have a vacancy clause. A vacancy clause states that if the home does not have a tenant or is vacant for a period of time, normally thirty to sixty days, the policy is void. Since you will not have a tenant the entire time you own the home, this is not the correct policy. A vacant home carries more risk than an occupied home. This is especially true if there is construction going on. Be sure your agent knows that you will be fixing and flipping and that no one will be living in the home. The correct policy is a builder's risk policy or a vacant property policy. The largest carriers of these policies are Foremost Insurance, Zurich, or Lloyd's of London. If it is not one of these, I would dig in a little to be sure you are covered correctly.

• For the most part, these policies are refundable; although you pay the entire premium up front, the unused premium can be refunded. So if you buy a six-month policy and it only takes you five months, you can cancel the policy and get a refund for one month. Be sure you are asking for a fully refundable policy and not a fully earned policy, which is not refundable.

• Most hard-money lenders will require replacement cost coverage. The two types of coverages in a policy are replacement cost and value. With a value policy, in the event of a loss, the insurance company will pay out based on the value of the damaged property. Take a roof for example. If it is damaged and needs to be replaced but is ten years old, a value policy will take a brand-new roof value and reduce that by an amount based on its age. If it is a thirty-year roof, they would take the full value and reduce that value by a third to account for the ten years of used life. With a value policy, you will never be paid enough to actually replace the damaged property. This is why hard-money lenders require replacement costs coverage and you should too. If that roof is ten years old and damaged, a replacement cost policy will provide the funds to replace the roof.

A typical rule of thumb for the correct insurance policy is an annual premium of about $1,000 a year for every $100,000 in coverage. That is the number I used in our example here. $3,000/12 = $250 per month.

Taxes. Unlike insurance, taxes are paid in arrears. For a fix-and-flip, it is possible that you will never make a payment for taxes. As the new owner, you are going to be responsible for an entire year of taxes even though you didn't own the home for the full year. For this reason, when you buy, the sellers give you a credit for the amount of time they owned the home in that year. For example, if you buy a home on March 15, you will see a credit at closing for taxes that will include January, February, and fourteen days of March. This will also be true when you sell. You will give a credit to the buyer to compensate them for the amount of time they did not own the home in that year. If taxes are currently due and not paid, the title company or attorney will deduct that from your proceeds at closing as well. Both insurance and taxes are taken care of in lump sums at the closing and not a monthly expense out of your pocket. I still include those two costs in this section because the amount of taxes and insurance that you will be responsible for is directly related to the amount of time you owned the property.

You can get the tax amount from the county or city that is charging the taxes. In most states, it would be the county treasurer. In this example the taxes are approximately $1,500 a year so I divided that by 12 to get our monthly tax responsibility of $125.

	# of Months
Interests Payments	$2,100 × 5 = $10,500
HOA	+ $0 × 5 = $0
Insurance	+ $250 × 5 = $1,250
Taxes	+ $125 × 5 = $625
Utilities	+ $250 × 5 = $1,250
Total	= $13,625

Utilities. You will be responsible for all utilities, including gas, electric, water, and sewer so you need to account for all of these.

Now we multiply each monthly expense by five and add everything together to get our total holding costs of $13,625 which we move into our MAO formula.

A seller concession is a legal bribe to buy the house, like an incentive to the buyer. We see concessions frequently in a buyer's market (when there are plenty of homes to choose from) and less often in a seller's market (when inventory tightens up). These concessions are usually seller-paid lender fees or closings costs, but they can also be money for a repair or improvement to the home, a home warranty policy, or anything else the buyer and seller agree to. In this case, I am going to budget for a $2,500 concession to help with closing costs.

I often say that outside your money source, your Realtor is your most important team member. They help find deals, they help liquidate deals, they help run comps, and they can get you into properties to keep up on the competition. If you find a good one, they are experienced and can help with your renovation plan too. They are truly valuable and need to be paid. I always encourage investors to pay their agents well and not beat them up on their commission, especially in the early stages of a relationship. If you find that you are buying and selling houses with the same agent, however, there does come a time when it is appropriate to negotiate their commission. I have never met an agent that won't have this conversation if you are both making money together. A typical listing fee is five percent to six percent of the purchase price. This commission will be split between your agent and the buying agent. In this example, I used $18,000 which is six percent of the ARV.

Finally, we need to subtract the closing costs when we sell. Remember, you have closing costs when you buy and closing costs when you sell. A good rule of thumb is to use one percent of the sale price for your budget. This should cover the title insurance and the closing fees.

Hold open. This is a great time to mention a hold open title policy or a binder depending on what part of the country you are in. You can find this in some states but not in others so be sure to check with your title company or attorney for options. A hold open or title binder is when the title company never issues the title policy to you when you buy the property. Instead, they leave the policy "open" and issue the policy when you resell the home. The benefit is that you will save a lot of money on the title premium when you sell the home to your new buyer. You will pay the premium only on the difference between what you paid for the house and what you are reselling it for instead of on the full amount you are selling the home for. The cost to do this is a small premium amount calculated from the original policy issued when you purchased the property. Most title companies will charge between 10 percent and 20 percent of the original premium for this benefit. Remember, when you buy a home, the seller most often will pay for this policy, and you would simply pay an additional 10 percent to 20 percent of that amount when you buy. The bottom line is this small premium amount on the front end can save you a lot of money on the back end, so it is worth asking about. One downside with this policy is it is only held open for a limited amount of time. I have not seen one held open longer than two years, but some are for as little as a year. If you don't resell the home in that amount of time, the policy will be issued, and you will lose that extra premium you paid and the benefit of the policy. One other downside is that you are forced to use the same title company that was used when you purchased the home. If you prefer to use a different title company when you sell, do not ask for a hold open policy.

After subtracting all the costs to do the flip, we will come up with our best offer. I normally would recommend that the investor run both the Max Loan Method and the Profit Method and offer the lower of the two, but either one works. The Max Loan Method is fast and easy but leaves some question on actual profits while the Profit Method takes time but is more accurate.

	$300,000 Sale Price (ARV)
−	$50,000 Profit
−	$6,700 CC (Purchase)
−	$50,000 Repairs
−	$13,625 Holding Costs
−	$2,500 Concessions
−	$18,000 Realtor fees
−	$3,000 CC (Sell)
=	156,175 Max Allowable Offer

When you compare the two offers on the same deal in our exercise, $153,300 for the Max Loan Method and $156,175 for the Profit Method, you see how close the two offers are. This is why hard-money lenders stick to the 70 percent rule. There is profit in the 70 percent rule.

Finally, I strongly encourage you to use a physical worksheet and a pen. Not a pencil. If you are using a pencil that erases or a spreadsheet, it is very easy to start changing numbers. It is tempting to assume you can get the project completed a little faster or maybe it will cost you less to do your rehab. The minute you start manipulating numbers to make it work is the minute you decide it is OK to lose money on the deal. Be sure to get this worksheet for free on the website for this book www.fundyourflip.com.

CASH TO CLOSE

Investors always want to know how much cash out of pocket is needed to close on the deal. We put together a Cash to Close worksheet found in the appendix to this book that walks you through the formula for a quick estimate. This is not an exact amount and is only getting you close. Once you have a deal under contract, your hard-money lender should be able to issue a disclosure or term sheet that will give you a better idea of what to expect. You can also use our online calculator to come up with this number as well as profits, payments, returns and more. Find that at www.fundyourflip.com.

On the surface, the cash to close formula is rather simple, but there are some nuances that need to be remembered or you will be surprised when you see that settlement statement. The formula is debits minus credits.

Credits on the settlement statement are any funds coming into the transaction on your behalf. Debits are funds that you need to pay out.

Calculate Debits

Closing Costs: _____ × _____ % + $2,500 = _____
                    Loan   Lender Points

Monthly Payment: _____ × _____ % / 12 months = _____
                      Loan   Lender Rate

Prepaid Items: _____ / 2 + $2,000 = _____
                 Monthly Payment

Total Debits: _____ + _____ + _____
                Purchase Price   Repairs   Closing Costs

+ _____ = _____
    Prepaid Items

Calculate Credits

Total Credits: _____ + _____ = _____
                    Loan   Earnest Money

Calculate Cash To Close

Cash To Close: _____ - _____ = _____
                    Debits   Credits

Let's go through an example to see how this works. I am going to stick with our same hypothetical deal with the $300,000 ARV and $50,000 for a rehab budget. I am also going to assume we were able to get the house under contract for our MOA using the Profit Method.

Calculate Debits

Closing Costs: __$210,000__ × __2__ % + $2,500 = __$6,700__
                    Loan   Lender Points

Monthly Payment: __$210,000__ × __12__ % / 12 months = __$2,100__
                      Loan   Lender Rate

We have covered both the closing costs and monthly payment in the MAO formulas in the previous section.

Prepaid Items: __$2,100__ / 2 + $2,000 = __$3,050__
                 Monthly Payment

The prepaid items consist of prorated interest and insurance. Remember, we talked about insurance being paid in advance and at the time of closing. This is also true with the first month interest payment. To calculate an estimate of prepaid items due at closing, divide the monthly mortgage payment in half. I do this knowing we are likely closing somewhere in the middle of the month, so I will owe roughly half a payment. I then add $2,000 to get me close to an insurance premium. Obviously, I can calculate both the actual insurance I will need to pay and the true prorated interest once I have a final loan amount, closing date, and insurance quote. For now, I am just trying to get close.

Total Debits:	$156,175	+	$50,000	+	$6,700	+	$3,050	=	$215,925
	Purchase Price		Repairs		Closing Costs	Prepaid Items			

My total debits are the combination of the purchase price, the construction costs, closing costs, and prepaid items. Because we are using our hypothetical example, I used our MOA assuming we got a contract on the home with the Profit Method and the same $50,000 in estimated repairs. We need to include the construction costs here because hard-money lenders will require an escrow for these funds that you can access through a draw process. That account will need to be funded at closing and will be included on the settlement statement.

Calculate Credits

Total Credits:	$210,000	+	$1,000	=	$211,000
	Loan		Earnest Money		

Credits are easy to calculate. It is the combination of your loan amount and the earnest money that you will be putting down. There are other credits—such as taxes, which we have discussed—that you will see on the settlement statement. You may also see other credits like concessions and utility credits, which you can include if you would like. For this formula, I choose to leave any of those miscellaneous credits off because they help act as a small buffer to any errors in my debit calculation. Feel free to add any credits in here that you want.

Cash to Close

Cash To Close:	$215,925	-	$211,000	=	$4,925
	Debits		Credits		

I start with debits and subtract credits because that is the best way to find an amount needed to close. As long as your final number is higher than zero, you will need that amount to get the deal closed. If you use this formula and you have a negative number, you will be getting money back at closing or your hard-money lender will need to lower the loan amount. Our example here shows that we will need $4,925 at closing on top of our earnest money.

To get this deal done, you would want to be sure you had money in a liquid account to cover the earnest money, the cash to close, and any liquid reserve requirement the hard-money lender has.

Chapter 5

Alternative Ways to Use Hard Money

Hopefully by now you can see how powerful hard money can be for both fixing and flipping homes and building a massive portfolio of cash flow. These are not the only two reasons real estate investors use hard money. Below are four more ways I see real estate investors use this amazing tool.

BRIDGE LOANS

"Bridge loan" has several different meanings. Usually, bridge loans are short terms loans to bridge a gap between where you are now and where you want to end up. A hard-money lender and commercial bridge lender can be used interchangeably. Many hard-money lenders on the residential side are bridge lenders for commercial loans. Basically, hard-money loans and bridge loans are the same tool; it is just that one term is used more in the residential world, and one is used more in the commercial space. Think nonconventional, nonbank short-term funding. Most of the time, bridge loans fall into the commercial bucket. It is getting very rare to see consumer bridge loans because of the strict regulation around this type of lending. Here are some of the common types of bridge loans used by commercial real estate investors.

STABILIZE A PROPERTY

Many commercial lenders require property to be fully stabilized before they will fund it. A fully stabilized property typically means it has an occupancy of 95 percent or higher and the ability to produce a debt service coverage ratio (DSCR) of 1.2 or better. The DSCR is what banks use to qualify a property for funding. It is the ratio of cash flow to the loan. A ratio of 1.2 means that the property produces 120 percent of the needed cash to make the payment on the loan. That means there will be 20 percent cash flow for the owner after the debt payments are made. Stabilized occupancy rates vary somewhat among lenders and with different asset types. A warehouse, for example, may have different occupancy guidelines from those of an apartment building.

If a real estate investor buys a property that does not qualify for a bank loan, they may bring in a hard-money or bridge lender to fund the project so they can stabilize it and get it ready for bank financing. Much like the BRRRR strategy, once the property is stable, the investor will refinance the loan and pay the bridge lender off.

REHAB A PROPERTY

Many times, a property will need to be rehabbed in order to stabilize it. Maybe some improvements will help the real estate investor increase rents or fill vacancies. Again, banks want assets with in-place cash flow, so their expectation is that the property is in good condition. The investor always has the option to fix-and-flip commercial properties exactly like investors do for residential property and will use a bridge lender to help fund those repairs.

TENANT IMPROVEMENTS

Commercial tenants will sometimes demand that work be completed in their space by the owner in order to sign a new lease. Owners are usually willing to make improvements for their tenants in exchange for a longer-term lease. I usually see leases to commercial tenants with improvements from five to ten years. We had a client purchase an old Safeway building and needed to shrink the space into smaller units to lease it. They signed a lease with a large fitness tenant, and the tenant paid a lease premium and signed a long-term lease in exchange for the demising wall and some improvements to their suite. By doing the improvements the tenant requested, this investor was able to double the value of the building. Obviously, it is worth doing the improvements to get a great tenant like this, but many banks will not fund tenant improvements. This is why hard-money or commercial bridge lenders are so important for commercial investors.

CITY APPROVALS

This is limited to land deals for the most part. If a real estate developer finds a piece of land they want to develop, they may need a bridge loan to help fund the purchase. Banks do not like land deals because land does not produce income. Banks also do not like funding construction loans unless they are fully approved and ready to go. A commercial bridge lender may be willing to help an investor fund the land while they work through the approval process. Once the approval is complete, it is much easier to get the bank construction loan, which can be used to pay off the bridge lender. These are riskier loans, and hard-money lenders don't like them for the same reasons banks don't. The difference is that your hard-money lender can think of ways to mitigate risks that are outside the normal lending box. They may be able to see the end or alternative strategies in case you are unsuccessful with your plan. Land loans will likely require a down payment—even with an aggressive hard-money lender—so be prepared to come up with some cash.

LIMIT DOWNPAYMENTS

This is exactly the same reason hard money is popular with the BRRRR strategy. By limiting your down payment, you keep more money in your pocket. It also allows you to fund larger deals that you may otherwise need a partner to do. Debt is almost always cheaper than giving up a piece of the deal to another investor, so savvy investors will use hard money to limit the down payment requirement and limit the number of partners they have, keeping more of the deal for themselves.

SPEED

Similar to a hard-money loan on the residential side, commercial sellers want to close fast. If the hard-money lender can see a clear way they will be paid back, like a refinance with a bank or a quick sale, they can help get you to the closing table much faster than other lenders. Most hard-money lenders that work with commercial properties fund deals on a regular basis that banks cannot get done in time. This allows the investor to close on the deal before they risk losing it, giving the bank the time it needs to close the loan. As soon as the bank is ready, the investor will refinance with the bank and pay off the hard-money bridge lender.

FLASH CASH

We don't see this as often as we used to, but it is useful from time to time. Flash cash is a loan that will be used for only a day or two at most. It is used to quickly fund a deal when you have another buyer lined up to purchase the property from you after you buy it from your seller. We call these wholesale deals.

A wholesale deal is when an investor gets a house under contract with the intent to sell it to another investor without doing any work. The wholesale investor, or wholesaler, will mark the property up slightly to make a profit. Because I am busy with Pine Financial, I no longer have the time to market for sellers and negotiate contracts. My time is better focused on helping our clients close their deals. That does not mean I am not continuing to build my real estate portfolio, however. I am very much in the market for new deals. Because I want deals but do not have the time to find them, I lean on wholesalers and am more than happy to pay their fee for their deals.

With that said, there was a time when I had more time and was actively marketing to sellers and meeting with them to buy their houses. All this activity created more opportunities than I could handle, so I would be the one who wholesaled deals to other investors. The last wholesale deal I sold to another investor made me a $15,000 profit for almost no work. This was a home run of a deal for me at the time. I understood real estate pretty well at this point in my career and had another investor call me for help. He wanted to partner with me on a deal he'd found. The problem for me was I had too many deals I was already working on and this one needed a lot of work. I told him I was not interested and suggested he wholesale it. I even offered to help him. He got frustrated and confused and told me he did not want to wholesale it. "Wholesaling is for the birds," he told me. I will never forget that. I decided to keep an eye on this deal in case he did not find a way to get it done. Because he was being greedy and rejecting my help, he ended up losing the deal. He was not able to close. I got in touch with the owner and met with them and put the house under contract. It was a complicated property with several additions that were not permitted and no heat in half the house. Even though I did not have time to take this project on, I knew there was profit here. I posted a message on my Facebook page and had a buyer the same day for a $15,000 profit. Once the deal closed, I reached out to the investor who'd introduced me to the deal and asked him if he would cash a check if I sent him one. Even though he fell out of contract, I would not have found the deal if not for him, and I felt like I owned him a bird dog fee. A bird dog fee is a fee (usually $1,000 to $2,000) paid to an investor for locating a deal but not negotiating it or getting it under contract. It is far less than a wholesale fee because the investor did not negotiate the contract or find the buyer. This investor was still bitter he lost the deal and told me not to worry about it. I sent him $2,000, and you know what? He cashed the check.

Wholesaling can be a great way to get started as a real estate investor because you quite literally do not need cash or credit to make money. There are several ways to conduct the wholesale transaction, including double closings, contract assignments, and entity transfers.

Double Closing

Because you cannot technically sell a property you don't own, in some cases you will be forced to close on a property before you can sell it to your buyer. A wholesaler may have a property under contract to buy and have a separate contract with a buyer to sell. In this example, they would need to close on the house, take title, and then they sell it for a profit. In these cases, the wholesaler may buy the house and sell the house in the same day or a day or two later.

There are two types of double closings. The first is a dry double closing, which was super popular when I got into this business in 2001. A dry double close is the double closing as I described above, but the funding from the end buyer is used to close both transactions. The way this works is the wholesaler will close on the sale of the property with their buyer before they close with the owner. That's right, they sign all the documents, including a deed to the house, with the end buyer before they own it! I know, sounds crazy! From there they may walk down the hall into another closing room and sign the documents with the owner. The end buyer's lender will wire in the money once both transactions are closed, and that money will be used to fund both closings. The title company records the deeds in the order required to make it a legitimate transaction. Because I was an investor long before I became a hard-money lender, I understood this transaction and would allow it if we were the lender. Many hard-money lenders would allow it. The key is to be sure the title company will not fund unless both transactions close. That gave us comfort in sending our money in and allowing it to be used for both closings. If the lender does not understand the dry double close or was not comfortable with it, the wholesaler would be forced to close with the owner first, which requires funding the purchase.

Aside from the lender not approving this transaction, many title companies across the country have stopped closing the dry double closings. I still see them from time to time, but they are rare. Also, many states have made them illegal. For this reason, almost all double closings are now what we call a wet double close. This just means that the wholesaler is required to fully fund their side of the transaction before they can sign a deed to a new buyer. If the wholesale investor has the cash, this is not a problem. If they don't have the cash, they will need a flash cash loan.

Flash cash normally costs the wholesaler between one and two points and no interest. It is just a fee to use the money for a day or two. These are extremely safe loans for the hard-money lender because the funding is released only if both sides of the transaction are complete. If the property is not resold to the new buyer, the initial closing can be unraveled, and the money will be returned to the hard-money lender. Because these loans are so safe, there is normally little to no qualifying for them. Although it is nice to know that flash cash is available, there is only one reason you would ever want to use it. That would be if the wholesaler does not want to disclose to the buyer how much they are making on the deal. In a double close situation, you do not need to disclose to your buyer what you are paying for the house. That will all come out when everything is recorded, but for the purpose of the transaction it is a way to hide the true numbers from your buyer. I believe in full transparency in business. I don't think you should ever conceal something like this, but I also know that some investors will not close on a deal if they think the wholesaler is making too much on it. To me that is crazy, but I know it happens. If you are concerned with that, it might make sense to double close, but keep in mind that with a double closing, you will have two sets of closing costs and will make less money. Outside of this one reason, there are better and cheaper ways to wholesale that will save you the hassle and the fees of a flash cash loan.

Assignment

A contract assignment is when you transfer your rights in a deal to someone else. As long as it is allowed in your contract with the owner of a house, you can transfer your rights and have someone else close on the deal instead of you. In this case, you would assign your contract to your buyer for a fee. They pay you your fee, you say thank you, and they close on the house. This is the simplest and cheapest way to wholesale a property.

Entity Transfer

An entity transfer is far more complicated but is a way to wholesale houses that are not assignable. Some sellers, especially banks, do not like contract assignments and will not allow them. For this strategy to work you will need to structure an entity. This could be an LLC, a corporation, or a trust. To keep this simple I will use the LLC for my example. If you as a wholesaler put a house under contract in the name of an LLC that you recently established, you could sell your ownership in that LLC for the wholesale fee. The investor who purchases the LLC can then close on the house in the name of the LLC. Once they own the house with the LLC, they can transfer title to the house to another entity if they choose. This is a bit more complicated, especially the first time you do it, because it involves setting up the company and transferring ownership, but it is a great way to avoid the double close and will save you thousands of dollars in extra closing costs or flash cash fees. You can learn more about this strategy on our blog at www.pinefinancialgroup.com.

IRA LOANS

Did you know you can own and finance real estate in your IRA? It is a bit more challenging than a normal real estate deal. Your IRA can sign on debt and take out a loan, but you individually cannot sign on or guarantee that debt. That debt belongs to the IRA alone. These are called nonrecourse loans. That only means that the lender cannot come after you personally for any default. The remedies to a default are limited to the IRA.

The process to do real estate deals inside your IRA starts by establishing a self-directed IRA account. Many brokerage houses will tell you the IRA with them is self-directed, but they are not. For them, it is considered self-directed because you get to choose which mutual fund to invest in. That is not self-directed. A true self-directed IRA allows you to buy anything you want as long as it is not prohibited by the IRS. This would include private alternative assets, such as the Pine Financial mortgage fund, syndications, crypto currency, precious metals, other commodities, and real estate. Once you have the property identified, the IRA will sign the contract and close on the deal. In most cases, this means an authorized signer for the custodian is the one who signs, not you personally.

As mentioned, if you want to use a loan to purchase a property in the IRA, you need to find a lender who will give the IRA a loan with no recourse to you. These lenders are difficult to find, but some hard-money lenders will do it. Some banks will do it too but only if the property is fully repaired and producing income to make the payments. Because hard money is a short-term solution, you will want to have a strategy to refinance the loan or sell the property for a profit. It is worth considering investing in real estate in your IRA because the profits can be huge and tax free.

MEZZANINE LOANS

Mezzanine loans are not something you hear a lot about as a real estate investor but can be one of the most powerful ways to finance your acquisition, if you can find a hard-money lender to do it. Mezzanine loans, or mezz loans, are loans that are not secured by the property but secured by the entity that owns or is purchasing the property. It is a hybrid between senior debt (such as a bank loan) and equity. This is more of an advanced strategy that you see in commercial real estate far more than you will find in residential. Most hard-money lenders will not do these loans, so I am only giving a brief overview.

Let's say you're going to buy a building for $1 million. The bank might like to see $300,000 in a down payment, but you only have $100,000. Where will you get the other $200,000? Some banks might allow you to put a junior lien behind their loan. A seller carryback is an example. Some banks, however, will require that all $300,000 come from equity from the owners or at least no lien on the property. In these cases, you could do a capital raise from private investors and give them a piece of the deal, which can be very expensive. Or, if you have a hard-money lender willing to do a mezz loan, they could step in. In that case they could possibly loan you the $200,000 secured by your member units in an LLC without any lien placed on the property at all. In this case, if you default on the loan, the lender will repossess the LLC, not the real estate. In that situation, you will lose the LLC and everything the LLC owns including the real estate. The lender would probably pay off the senior debt, but they would have all the same options as the owner of the LLC had before the default.

As a lender, I don't love these types of loans. It is far less transparent than a lien on a property, and I could see a challenge with repossessing the member units. As a borrower, it could be risky too. Because there's no foreclosure process to repossess the asset, you will have limited time to rectify a default with zero redemption rights. These loans will carry higher rates and fees to compensate for the added risk. Mezz loans are only used by the most sophisticated borrowers and lenders.

Chapter 6

Gotcha! Things to Watch Out for with Hard-Money Loans

Here are some things other than hidden fees, which we have already covered, to watch out for when considering a hard-money loan.

PERSONAL GUARANTEE

A personal guarantee is you as an individual guaranteeing the loan. This means you and your personal balance sheet are liable if there is any loss on the loan to the lender. If you default on the loan, the lender will first try to recoup what is owed by repossessing and liquidating the property. If there is still money due after that, they will look to you personally to cover it. If you do not, they could pursue a personal judgment. Although it is possible to get a loan with no personal guarantees, like the IRA loan, it is rare. Guarantees are extremely common with residential real estate and are becoming more common with commercial. Unless the loan is to an IRA, every hard-money lender I know requires this now. The national gurus and late-night infomercials will tell you to never guarantee a loan because it is higher risk, but the reality is you'd better be prepared for it.

With all this said, it is my experience that if you are willing to work with the lender to help them avoid a loss, they may be flexible with that personal guarantee. Obviously if you do guarantee the loan, be prepared to pony up, but also work with the lender as much as you can. It is expensive to pursue personal guarantees, and often what judgment a lender gets will not be collectible, so the last thing a lender wants is to try to collect from you personally. I mention this only to be clear that if you do run into trouble on a project, let your lender know right away and try to work with them so you all can come out of the deal.

SLOW DRAWS

A draw is when the lender releases money on the loan to cover construction. As you progress through the project, the lender will advance funds to you or your contractor. Lenders do it this way to protect themselves and their investors. Because hard-money lenders base their loan decision on the value of the property after it's repaired, they need to do their best to ensure that you repair the property. Controlling the funds and releasing money with progress is the best way to do this.

The problem for you as the real estate investor is when the lender is slow to release this money. You have contractors that need to be paid and material to buy. Without a steady flow of funding, your project will stall, and contractors could walk off the site, costing you thousands of dollars. And to add insult to injury, often you are paying interest on this money even if it has not been released to you. It works this way because construction money is supposed to be set aside in a trust account for you and your project. Because the money is set aside for you in a separate account, the hard-money lender no longer has access to it, so they need to charge interest on it. What I have seen is even though the hard-money lender is charging you interest on this money, they don't always set it aside for you. They plan to fund these draws with other money, which may or may not be available for you when you are ready. That is a big problem. When you interview hard-money lenders, be sure to dig into the draw process and be sure you can get the money in a timely manner. It is also a good idea to have some reserves set aside so you can pay your contractors when they invoice you and have your lender reimburse you. This way, your contractor is not waiting on your lender, and the project can continue forward.

AUTOMATIC EXTENSIONS

Most hard-money lenders build in extensions, which can be very expensive. This could include extension fees and an increased interest rate. Some hard-money lenders are pretty flexible with extensions, and some will hammer you if you need one. I know of one lender in Denver who makes a major piece of revenue on their extension fees and penalties. This lender lures investors in by promising low interest rates and low fees. What they don't talk about is the extremely short term of the loan. They will write a loan with a term that is not sufficient to complete the project with the idea of charging their borrower excessive fees and interest once the loan matures. This is sad because most investors do not budget for this nor are they aware of what's going on. Be sure you understand the amount of time you have when borrowing from a hard-money lender and what the consequences are if you need more time.

COMMITMENTS THAT CANNOT BE FULFILLED

Some hard-money lenders, especially the smaller ones, commit to loans before they have the money available. They may be expecting another loan to pay off to free up the cash or could be hoping to raise the money before closing. The worst part about this is they don't tell you! Real estate transactions are based on deadlines. If you miss a deadline, you could lose the deal.

We recently helped a client with $10,000 of earnest money at risk whose private-money lender fell through three days before closing.

At least he gave this real estate investor three days to find a solution and did not wait until the day of closing. This was enough time for us to step in and help save the deal. Had we not closed on this deal on the closing date, the investor would have lost her earnest money and lost the deal. The seller is a popular wholesaler who is known for keeping earnest money and reselling homes to increase profits. Be sure you are working with a reputable hard-money lender and that when they make a commitment to you, they can execute.

MARKETING PLOYS

We have been successful focusing on transparency. We don't use bait and switch, teaser rates, or hidden fees, and our clients love it and stick with us. I find it hard sometimes to compete for new investor business because some investors are so focused on chasing the best pricing that they get sucked into some of the ploys other hard-money lenders use. Because every hard-money lender has different pricing structures, different ways to do business, and different loan guidelines, borrowers have a hard time comparing loans; they're apples and oranges. So how do real estate investors know what loan is best for them? We all want to save money, of course, but more than that, we don't want to be taken advantage of. Here are some of the most common marketing ploys being used by hard-money lenders.

TEASER RATES

These come in a couple of different forms. They can be a starting rate that adjusts after a set period of time or can be a low-rate loan with a short term and high extension costs. Although adjustable rates are not very common in the hard-money lending space, they are something you should be aware of. Adjustable rates are tied to an index with a margin attached. The most common index used is the Wall Street Journal Prime Rate, or simply the prime rate. The margin is a fixed rate that is added to the index. So you have a rate of four percent over prime, you would add four percentage points to the prime rate to get the interest rate that you will pay. If they promise a low starting rate and then a rate that adjusts, they will only advertise the low rate so be careful. Once that rate starts to adjust it is only going up! The other teaser rate ploy is a super short-term loan like four to six months. After that, the rate skyrockets. Most investors are confident they can be out of a loan in four to six months until their contractor takes a trip or leaves the job site. Or the house does not sell as fast as they hoped. It was Mike Tyson that famously said, "Everyone has a plan until they get punched in the face." The teaser rate hard-money lenders are counting the project taking longer than expected.

JUNK FEES

So the hard-money lender is promising a half point or one point origination fee, so you call for more information. They seem legitimate, so you commit to working with them on a fix-and-flip. You get within a few days of closing and finally see the term sheet. It discloses the document preparation fee you did not hear about along with the large exit fee and maybe a few other fees such as large underwriting or inspection fees. This lender got you in with the promise of a low origination but surprised you with the other fees not usually discussed. Almost all hard-money lenders have some kind of administrative fee, which is used to help cover overhead, but that fee should be a single fee, and it should be reasonable. Oh, and it should be disclosed up front. If the hard-money lender is not providing you a term sheet or a fee disclosure of some kind, they may be trying to hide some fees until you are closer to closing.

LTC/LTV REQUIREMENTS

Many hard-money lenders have strict loan-to-cost and loan-to-value requirements and offer better rates for lower loan-to-cost or loan-to-value loans. They won't promote the higher loan rate though. They advertise the lowest rates they can offer and when your appraisal comes in, that rate changes. They base the interest rate you pay on the final loan-to-cost or loan-to-value, not the best rates they can offer.

BAIT AND SWITCH

Almost all marketing ploys come down to the bait and switch. Promise one thing and deliver another. The business model of these lenders is to get you in the door and then promise to be transparent on future deals. Or they feed on new investors and never intend to deliver what you expect. Be very careful here and ask your lender a lot of questions to be sure you are both comparing apples to apples and getting what you expect.

Chapter 7

Questions to Ask Your Lender

The best way to get the best loan and stay safe is to understand the loan and the lender. Although difficult, you want to try to compare apples to apples. What makes one loan better in your situation than another? Here are the top eight questions to ask your hard-money lender.

ARE YOU A LENDER OR A BROKER?

You want to know if they are brokering somebody else's money or if they have direct access and control of the money. I am not saying one is better than the other, but if they are brokering money, they are adding fees to the money source, which could make it more expensive for you. They also do not make the decisions. I know some hard-money brokers, similar to bank vice presidents, who will tell you whatever you want to hear. They might even supply you with your preapproval letter before they know you're approved. This is a dangerous game.

Although I would say in most cases you want to deal directly with the lender, sometimes you need a broker. Hard-money brokers know the market and know lenders. They understand which loan is best for certain situations and can help direct you to the best loan. It might make sense to pay a little more to have a professional on your side.

WHERE IS THE MONEY COMING FROM?

When dealing with a direct lender, you will want to know where their money is coming from. This might be the most important question you ask any private-money lender or hard-money lender. Many hard-money lenders are small companies loaning out their own money and maybe the money of some close friends. Some use debt and some have large mortgage funds of private investors. Here are some potential risks depending on where the money is coming from:

Individual Retirement Account

If the money is coming from an IRA of an investor, there could be delays with closing. Some IRA administrators take longer than expected, and I have heard many times of the funding coming after closing. This can create tremendous stress because if you don't hit your closing deadline, the seller does not need to close at all.

Debt

Another concern could be if the money is coming from an outside debt source, such as a bank loan or line of credit. The reason this can be concerning is that they have specific guidelines that can, and do, change. If you are approved for your loan with your hard-money lender and the guidelines change on their line of credit, they may be forced to deny the loan. I hope that does not happen when you are expecting them to come through for you. It is also possible that the hard-money lender receives a margin call from their bank. A margin call is when the bank asks for the borrower to reduce the balance on the line of credit. If the bank feels the underlying collateral—in this case it would be the loans the lender has made—has decreased in value, it may ask that the hard-money lender pony up some cash and reduce the loan amount. This became extremely relevant in March of 2020 when COVID-19 hit the scene. More than half of the hard-money lenders I know had to stop loaning money during this time. Their wells went dry. This included loans in their current pipeline, which severely hurt their business but was great for lenders without the margin call risk. Those lenders continued to lend through the COVID-19 pandemic and received a high level of calls from clients who were unable to close on current deals with their current hard-money lender.

Mortgage Fund

If the hard-money lender has a mortgage fund, they have the most control of the money. They most likely will approve, underwrite, and service the loans in-house and are a lender that you can count on. The two downsides are they might be a tad more expensive because private money is normally more expensive than bank money and that money is finite, so they could run out. You have to hope the lender is transparent and does not commit to a loan they cannot fund. We have elected to lean heavily on our mortgage funds, helping our investors earn high and steady passive returns, and supplement with private note buyers and small bank lines. This way, we have the capacity and liquidity to fund the deals we commit to.

WHAT ARE YOUR RATES AND FEES, AND DO THOSE CHANGE FOR DIFFERENT BO-RROWERS?

This has got to be the most obvious question you want to ask your lender. The key here is trying to figure out the bait and switch and any teaser rate they are promising and whether the terms of the loan change based on your experience level or down payment. How long will it take them to get you a term sheet, and will that term sheet disclose all the hidden fees? Dig in here and be sure to ask what the hidden fees are.

WHAT ARE YOUR DOWN PAYMENT REQUIRE-MENTS?

Here is where we really start to dig into comparing apples to apples. We have a couple of different loan products to help our real estate investors succeed, and those loans are priced differently. This is mostly because of the down payment requirement. If you're looking for a higher leverage loan, you will pay more for it because there is more risk for the lender. When you hear really low rates being advertised for hard-money, there are probably large down payment or capital requirements. I wonder sometimes why you would put so much money down to get a hard-money loan when you can go to the bank and get rates at half of what they are offering. One of the biggest advantages to hard money is the high leverage.

HOW DOES YOUR DRAW PROCESS WORK?

What I am looking for here is how quickly the money will come in so I can pay my contractors. I also want to know the process and how challenging it is to make the request. One important thing for you as the borrower to understand is that the hard-money lender is supposed to have a separate trust account set up for this money. A trust account is the type of account used by attorneys and title companies to hold other people's money. Because these accounts are used to hold someone else's money in trust, they are structured to protect the funds in the account from any lawsuits against the signor of the account. So if you deposit your earnest money into a title company and the title company loses a lawsuit, there is no risk to your earnest money as long as it is in their trust account. If the hard-money lender just deposits that money into a normal bank account, it is possible for a creditor of your hard-money lender to get ahold of your cash. Not only is the trust account extremely important to protect you as the borrower, but you also want to make sure that the money actually moves into that account and is available for you to draw on. Many hard-money lenders will charge you interest on these escrow money but only fund it once requested. This can create huge issues for you if there is ever a liquidity issue with that hard-money lender. It would almost be a Ponzi scheme by using funds from other deals to fund your draws. That type of scheme ends badly when you need a draw and there is no money to fund it. Other than broken promises with closing, this is the number one reason borrowers of other hard-money lenders come to us for help.

WHAT IS THE TERM, AND WHAT HAPPENS IF WE EXCEED THE TERM?

"Loan to own," as the saying goes. Some hard-money lenders want to do shorter-term loans so they can create problems for you. When a problem is created, it will cost you money to fix it, which means more money for the hard-money lender. I would be sure they are giving you enough time to complete your project and understand the process if you go over that time. And have a plan if you do exceed the timeline.

HOW LONG HAVE YOU BEEN DOING THIS?

Obviously, you don't want to be the hard-money lender's first borrower. The more experience they have, the more issues they have run into and the easier it is for them to help you if you need it. There is no huge barrier of entry into this business, so you will see hard-money lenders enter and exit the industry regularly. Because there is turnover, it is possible to be dealing with new hard-money lenders. Try to focus on the experienced ones with the best reputations.

CAN YOU SHARE SOME REFERENCES?

Speaking of reputations, it is always good to get references. You could simply ask for a few references or you could ask for the most recent three references. The hard-money lender may or may not give you this information for privacy reasons of their borrower, but if you ask for the last three deals they've closed, they will not be able to cherry pick their favorite clients. Once you get the references, try to get an address for the deal they funded and look up the recordings for that property to be sure that they actually funded the deal. From there, you can call the borrower to get their opinion of the hard-money lender. You may want to know how many of their deals the hard-money lender has funded and what problems they've had with that hard-money lender. You can ask them many of these same questions and get answers from an outside prospective.

Chapter 8

Top Investor Mistakes

Being a real estate investor for more than two decades, I have seen and made many mistakes. As a hard-money lender, I see many more. As a hard-money lender working exclusively with real estate investors, these are the top ten mistakes I see investors making.

BUYING WITHOUT A CLEAR EXIT STRATEGY

The saying is "you make your money when you buy." That is true, *but* you need to have a strategy to get paid that money. Hard-money lenders expect and probably demand it. The exit strategy is what you are going to do with the property. For a single-family home, it could be simple, such as a fix-and-flip or a rehab and refinance, or it could be more complicated, such as a lot split, a development, or an assemblage. For commercial, you could be looking at a conversion, a repurpose, or a thousand other strategies. No matter what your plan, just have a plan. It is a good idea to also have a plan B. And maybe a C. Real estate investments are great but don't always go as planned, so be sure you are prepared.

PAYING CASH

I was in the office working on a loan to help one of our real estate investor clients and a call came in. "Kevin, can you take a call from the *Las Vegas Review Journal*?"

"Who?" I asked.

"The *Las Vegas Review Journal*," she said.

What in the heck is this is? I thought to myself. "Um, OK" and the call came over."

"Good afternoon, this is Kevin."

"The same Kevin that thinks owning property free and clear is a mistake?"

Wow. What a start. Turns out I got interviewed and quoted in the *Las Vegas Review Journal* because of my strong opinion about this topic.

If you are in the financial growth phase of your life, which I assume you are or you would not be reading this, owning property free and clear is a mistake. Or at least it is slowing you down. If you are in retirement or close to it, or possibly just don't have the time to focus on your investments, then it could be smart to eliminate debt, but otherwise it is much smarter to have some kind of leverage. I believe this for two reasons:

1. Spreads

The obvious reason for growth is you can probably earn a higher return on your investment than you would pay in interest on your loan. Banks are important, and when they focus on lending and not making speculative investments, they tend to do well. Banks bring in money from you and me in checking and savings accounts, they supplement that with money from other banks or the government, and then they lend that money back to you and me in the form of credit cards, auto loans, personal loans, home loans, and other loans at higher interest rates. Banks make money borrowing money at a low rate and loaning it back out at a higher rate. Why can't we do that? This is called a spread. If you can borrow at five percent and earn eight percent, your net is a three percent return with none of your own money. This is one way the rich grow their wealth.

2. Litigation

We live in a litigious world. I hate it, but it is reality. I know there is a place for personal injury attorneys, and they play an important role, but it's also important to understand they get paid to sue people. We should do what we can to protect ourselves the best we can.

As previously mentioned, most of these attorneys get paid on a contingency fee. This means they are paid on the amount of money they are able to collect for their client. The amount they *collect*, not the amount they win in a case. So if you get into a car accident or a skiing accident, the attorney will first look for assets they can collect on before they take the time to sue you. It is one thing to win a lawsuit, but a totally different thing to collect once you win. Because these attorneys are not paid for winning, they won't sue someone they cannot collect from, unless they are focused on the insurance company, of course. Real estate is the most transparent asset that exists. Attorneys can find every property you own and all the loans and liens recorded against those properties in the time it takes you to make dinner. If you own property free and clear, you have a target on your back.

OFFERINF TO PAY CASH WHEN YOU DON'T HAVE IT

Sounds funny, right? Making an offer on a house that you cannot perform on? It is more common than you think, especially when the market gets hot and deals are harder to come by. Real estate investors try to do anything they can to make their offer stand out, including offering to pay cash when they don't have it. The thought is that cash at the closing table is cash, no matter where it comes from, and if they have a hard-money lender in tow, they have the cash. Heck, I know real estate agents and Realtors who will advise their clients to do this.

The problem is that the hard-money lender will most likely require a lender title policy. They would be crazy not to. There are two types of title policies. The owner policy, which is normally paid for by the seller, which insures you, the new owner, against any defects on title. Basically, it is insurance that when you buy the property you are buying what you think you are buying. If something comes up like a challenge of previous ownership, for example, you have an insurance policy that you can make a claim on that will protect you. The lender policy protects the lender by insuring their lien. Title companies are only supposed to offer the lender policy if the contract allows for it. So if you offer all cash, there is a decent chance the title insurance company will not offer the lender policy and the hard-money lender will not provide the loan. That little idea of offering all cash when you don't have it made it so you cannot close.

The best way to write your offer when using hard money is to list the hard money in the financing section of the contract. If you think that you lose some advantage by disclosing this, you could offer cash as long as you have a provision in the contract that allows you to use a loan. Most investors will add this to an additional provision section and say something like, "Buyer reserves the right to finance the purchase with a loan as long as it does not affect the seller's net proceeds." If you put this clause or something similar somewhere in your contract, the title company will offer the policy needed for your lender to offer the loan.

PUTTING ADDITIONAL CAPITAL INTO A BAD DEAL

This is the classic story of trying to save earnest money. For newer investors, I would suggest never allowing earnest money to go hard. That just means that all your contract contingencies expire and your earnest money is no longer refundable. When earnest money is hard, if you don't close on the contract, the seller keeps your money. It is easy to keep earnest money safe with solid contingencies in your contract. This is why using a reputable Realtor is smart. There are times, however, when your earnest money needs to go hard to get a deal, as when dealing with wholesalers, for example. I will say this again: do not do this if you are new to the business!

What I see is that investors will put a house under contract with hard earnest money and then come to us to finance it. We do our diligence and determine that it is not a profitable deal and suggest they back out. But because the earnest money is hard, they decide to close, essentially putting good money after bad, attempting to save their earnest money and not take a small loss on the property. I have not followed up every time this has happened, but when I have, without exception, the investor regretted doing the deal. The $5,000 or $10,000 loss they would have taken had they backed out turned into a $20,000 or $30,000 loss. I think the saying is "live to fight another day." Or "It is OK to lose the battle but win the war." You cannot win the war if you are killed on a single deal. Sometimes it is better to cut your loss, lick your wounds, get better, and move on.

UNDERESTIMATING HOLDING AND CLOSING COSTS

I hope that after reading this book, you will not make this mistake. Underestimating these two numbers will certainly affect the profit you were expecting. Closing costs are underestimated when using hard money for a few reasons. Obviously, it is more expensive, so if you budget for bank financing and then go with hard money, your profit will look different. But outside of that, as we discussed, some hard-money lenders will charge you more than you were expecting, so be sure to understand what you are getting into when you run your numbers on your deal.

Also, the holding costs can be missed in your numbers if you forget something. Items such as utilities, insurance, and prorated taxes are all missed by investors. This is why I highly recommend using the MAO formula for your deals. This worksheet is part of the appendix to this book. You can also download your free copy at www.fundyourflip.com.

BEING BROKE AND STINGY

You watched that show on HGTV and then the late-night infomercial. You saw the fancy car and the big house. You learned that you don't need money to do real estate deals and apparently it is easy and will make you rich! You start to study and learn, and you gain confidence to start making offers. You are thinking of wholesaling houses to start because you don't have cash in the bank, and heck, you are just getting started. You know wholesaling does not require cash and can be done risk-free. And then it happens. You get a deal under contract. After running the numbers, you see the big profit that can be made if you fix-and-flip, and you want it. You could easily wholesale this house and make a quick $5,000 or even more, but you want the payday. You want to fix and flip it like they did on TV.

The experts told you that if you find a great deal, the money will find you (something I disagree with, by the way), so you decide to do the deal. You call your hard-money lender, and they love the deal but cannot finance it because you don't have the reserves in the bank in case there is a problem. Most hard-money lenders will require some liquidity even if they fund 100 percent of the deal. Instead of going back to your plan of wholesaling, you call another lender, and then another. All of a sudden, you are up against a closing date without time to wholesale, and you lose the deal and your earnest money. Your projected $50,000 profit turned into the loss of your earnest money.

It would be foolish to take on a fix-and-flip with no reserves. Even the best and most experienced real estate investors go over budget or take longer than they thought to rehab or sell the house. You don't see this reality on reality TV. Reserves in the bank is the only way to keep you safe when the plan does not go to plan. In this example, you lost a wholesale fee of at least $5,000 because you were stingy and wanted the entire profit for yourself. In this case, it would have been much better to wholesale the deal or possibly bring in a partner to share the profit with to get the deal done. Once you have the cash in the bank, then start flipping on your own. As we have all heard a million times: 50 percent of something is far better than 100 percent of nothing.

BEING EMOTIONALLY ATTACHED TO A HOUSE

This is one that I can understand. It is very difficult to keep emotion out of this business, especially when you are getting started. These emotions can cost you big, so be careful. There are two times that emotions can get you in trouble as a real estate investor. One is the feeling for the real estate itself. If you enjoy the transformation of the property, you could easily make improvements that are not in the best interest of the bottom line. If you like a specific slab of granite or a light fixture that would look amazing, but these selections put you over your budget, stick to the option that keeps you on budget. You are not remodeling your dream home; you are trying to make a profit! I understand being proud of the transformation, which you should be, but do not do that to the detriment of your wallet.

The other time emotions are dangerous is when you are putting the house under contract. This can be true when selling, but is especially true when you are buying. Maybe it is chasing earnest money, which we discussed, or you are just desperate for a deal. "I need to keep my guys busy" is one I hear all the time. It could be the excitement of the potential profit and then you find something in your inspection that changes the numbers, and you physically feel the disappointment. There is a ton of emotion around real estate and money. Keep these emotions out of your business and stay safe. Use the MAO sheet and always stick to your numbers!

INCORRECT USE OF ENTITIES

I see many mistakes when it comes to the use of entities, especially in states that allow the single member entity. I am not an attorney and am not giving legal advice. Every person or investor has a unique situation and legal advice should come only from an attorney who understands your specific situation. This is only my understanding of how these entities work and what I see on a day-to-day basis. Here are the top mistakes made with use of entities:

Deeding a Property into an Entity Before You Have Your Permanent Loan in Place

As we discussed earlier in the book, hard money is an excellent way to buy rental property. You purchase a property with hard money, reducing the amount of out-of-pocket cash needed, rehab it, rent it, and then refinance it. The issue is that conventional lenders cannot loan to an LLC or corporation, so if you deed the property out of your name or buy the property in the name of the entity, you will have trouble with the refinance. When using the BRRRR strategy, it is always best to get through your financing completely and then deed the property into an entity if that is what you want to do.

Not Using One

As discussed, if your exit strategy is to refinance your hard-money loan, then you should keep the property in your personal name until the permanent loan is in place. This is true only for properties you plan to refinance with a conventional loan. If you are planning to flip the house or have another strategy in mind, buying property in an entity and not your personal name probably makes a lot of sense. Again, I recommend you check with an attorney, but I would be shocked if any attorney advised you to do business in your personal name.

No Operating Agreement

In many states, you can have an LLC with one member. That member is most likely you. There are some big advantages to doing it this way, but it is all based on taxes and ease of business. For reasons I cannot go into in this book, I would always suggest at least two members in an LLC. Check out our YouTube video "What Is A Charging Order?" https://youtu.be/lmOIyrM5_p0. Or go to our channel and search for "charging order" www.youtube.com/pinefinancial That aside, what I find funny is that even though you are the only member, you still need to have an Operating Agreement for your entity. An Operating Agreement discloses to the title company and the lender who the owners are and who has authority to sign on behalf of the business. It is also good practice to legitimize your company. I know it sounds funny to have a formal agreement agreeing with yourself, but, yes, you need it.

Not a Separate Business

As a hard-money lender, we are looking at bank statements for proof of liquidity. It is far more common than I wish to admit to have real estate investors living out of the business account. Fast food, gas station coffee, nights out—all on the business account. A $10 McDonald's charge is not a business meeting. These types of transactions are commingling business and personal funds and make it easy for an attorney to pierce the LLC or corporation, providing zero asset protection. What is the point of creating and managing the entity if it provides no protection? The way to keep business and personal funds separate is to issue a draw from the company into your personal account, entering it as a dividend or draw on the company books, and then using your personal account to buy the Big Mac.

BITING OFF MORE THAN YOU CAN CHEW

I am only half joking when I say that probably the worst thing that can happen to you is for you to make a bunch of money on your very first deal. Now, I don't necessarily want you to lose money, but making a good chunk on your first deal can become problematic for some investors. We all know what happens when we see success on our first try. We start thinking we're invincible and what we just accomplished is easy and repeatable. We could do it again and more, and we cannot get hurt. At that point, we have no foundation and instead of doing one deal, we try to take on two or three or even four, long before we are ready. And that's when it happens. The house of cards comes tumbling down. I know of many once successful investors no longer doing deals for this exact reason. This mistake more than any other is the one I see turning more full time real estate investors into someone working for a paycheck. They take on more than they can handle. This is very, very sad and very common. No, I'm not saying I want you to lose money on your first deal—although that would not be a terrible thing if you stick with it—I just don't want you to make very much. I'm only kidding, but my point is to start with a solid foundation, stay humble, and grow at a safe pace.

NO ASSET PROTECTION

"It is not if; it's when." I did not believe it. The longer you are in this business, the more you will hear this. All successful people get sued at some point. I try so hard to be honest and do the right thing, and I have been sued. Some people see what you have and want a piece. One of my closest friends, Shawn, got sued for the first time a few years ago. I remember sitting down with him as he dealt with the situation. He is a developer and built a house on an existing foundation. There was some small movement in the house, which can be normal, and the homeowner was upset. Shawn offered to fix it, but they wanted blood. They had an attorney who needed to be paid. They came at Shawn hard! This really upset him. He is the nicest, most honorable guy I know. He was willing to do anything he could to be sure his buyer was satisfied. He hates conflict and was not ready. We talked through the situation over a beer, and I just put it out there. "Shawn, you'd better get used to this." He was stunned, but I continued. "When you are successful, you get sued. It is not personal." He has been sued a handful of times since then and understands now that it is part of business and still thanks me for that conversation. No longer does he let it bring him down.

We have already talked about entities. Different entities can provide different levels of asset protection, but your asset protection plan does not start or end with an entity. That is just one piece of an overall plan. Insurance, transparency, a good attorney, and just flat-out doing the right thing are all important pieces of a plan to protect your assets. The use of entities is important, but don't let not having an entity stall your success. It is OK to learn what you can, make offers, and do some deals before you worry too much about your entity. Most, or maybe all, attorneys will disagree with me on this one and this is my opinion alone, but I would not spend too much time or money trying to protect assets that I don't even have yet. Maybe start with a good insurance agent, get a deal or two behind you, and then create your overall asset protection plan with entities. But no matter what, have a plan.

NOT TAKING ACTION

Hands down, by far, no question, the biggest mistake investors make is not taking any action at all. A lot of the common mistakes I see investors make that result in loss of money are after they are doing deals. Trust me on this: money is much easier to make the second time around. So I recommend focusing on making money first and then focus on mistakes that can create a loss of it. The first and most lethal mistake you can make is never making money in the first place. We teach a lot of classes in the markets we work in, and we have annual real estate investor conferences and monthly networking meetings. I love seeing the same people over and over. We become friends, we get to know each other, and we care about each other's success. What bothers me is people coming out to the meetings, learning everything they can, and never buying a house. The reason for this is fear of a mistake. I understand that, but what's the bigger mistake? You and I both know you're going make mistakes. So why let something you already know is going to happen stop you from trying. Expect it! When you try, you will learn and you will build momentum, and then, you will succeed!

Hard-Money Glossary

70 percent rule: This is the rule that real estate investors use to quickly analyze real estate opportunities. The rule is that purchase and the repairs should be less than or equal to 70 percent of the ARV. Hard-money lenders usually cap their loan at 70 percent of the ARV because a 30 percent margin is both profitable and conservative.

After repaired value (ARV): In most cases, this is the value of a residential property once all the rehab is complete. Some investors call this the "retail" value. In commercial, it is more commonly known as stabilized value, but sometimes you will hear the term ARV for a highly stable commercial property.

Arrears: This is when a payment is due the period after a product or service has been earned. For interest arrears, the payment is due the month after interest is earned. In another example, property taxes paid in arrears when they are due the following year they accrue.

As-is value: As a Realtor or investor, the as-is value is normally the value of the real estate as it currently sits, with no improvements. For lenders, though, the as-is value is the appraised value or the purchase price, whichever is less.

Balloon: A balloon is the last day of a term loan. It means that the loan is due in full on that date. Most hard-money loans have balloons, so you should expect to pay the entire loan off in a short period of time. Most investors pay off their hard-money loans with a refinance or by selling the real estate.

Bridge loan: Any loan that bridges a gap. This is an extremely broad term with multiple meanings. Some examples of bridge loans are a shorter-term hard-money loan for a fix-and-flip, the BRRRR strategy, funding for a fast close, a loan for land before a bank will finance construction, and a commercial project that needs more income before a lender will touch it. A bridge loan is any loan that is used on a short-term basis as a means to an end.

Closing costs: Costs that must be paid to close a transaction. There are two sets of closing costs.

- o   Closing costs when you buy. These include loan origination fees, title insurance, title fees, appraisal fees, HOA transfer fees, insurance, and other miscellaneous costs.

- o   Closing costs when you sell. These include real estate commissions, title insurance, tax prorations, final utilities payments, transfer fees, title fees, and other miscellaneous costs.

Closing statement: Also known as the settlement statement, this is the document that discloses how the title company is handling the funds. It details where the money for the transaction is coming from and where it is going.

Combined loan-to-value (CLTV): Combined loan-to-value is the ratio that accounts for all the loans on the property, not just the first mortgage. It is calculated by taking the sum of all the debt against the property and dividing it by the value.

Deed of trust: This is the lien on the property that pledges to the lender the property as collateral for the loan. It gets recorded with the county and gives the public notice of the loan. These are used only in states that allow them. Hard-money lenders will use this document when possible because it is much easier to foreclose with a deed of trust than a mortgage. A deed of trust is often confused with the deed to the property. The deed of trust is not a deed. It is only a lien giving the lender certain rights to the property in specific circumstances, like being able to force place insurance, make repairs if needed, or foreclose if the borrower stops making payments.

Earnest money: This is the deposit given by the buyer of a house as a deposit. Its purpose is to prove intent and give the seller comfort that the buyer will close on the transaction. If the buyer does not close, the seller may be able to retain this to compensate them for their damages, but a good agent should be able to protect this money with a solid contract.

Escrow: This can have multiple meanings.

- Title escrow is when a third party holds funds and documents in trust to facilitate a closing. Escrow is open when the property goes under contract with a seller and a buyer, and the escrow company starts to collect documents and funds. Once all documents and money are in escrow, the transaction is complete, and the escrow company will close escrow by recording documents and disbursing funds and documents to the parties. This is known as the closing.

- Construction escrow is when a title company, attorney, or lender holds funds in a trust account that will be released in draws as construction is completed.

- Mortgage escrow is when a mortgage company sets up a separate account for the borrower to pay taxes and insurance. With each payment, they collect a small amount and use that money to make the payments for these two expenses. That way, the borrower can have one monthly payment and will not need to worry about these larger expenses when they come due. A full payment with a mortgage escrow is known as PITA (principal, interest, taxes, and insurance). It would be unusual for a hard-money lender to collect a mortgage escrow.

- Other escrow can be any time an attorney, title company, or other third party holds funds or documents in trust. Some common escrows that we see are holding funds for code violation corrections or other needed repairs, disputed funds until there is a resolution, or important documents that neither party wants the other party to have unless there is a default.

Exit strategy: As an investor, the exit strategy is the plan for your profit. This could be something simple, such as a fix-and-flip or use of the BRRRR strategy and refinance the loan, or it could be more complicated, such as splitting a lot or combining parcels for a larger project. When your hard-money lender asks about your exit strategy, tell them your profit plan, but make sure it includes a way to pay them back.

Hard costs: These are the costs that improve a project that are tangible as opposed to intangibles such as architectural plans, testing, or permitting.

Hard earnest money: This is when your earnest money is no longer refundable and will be lost if you do not close on the project. This occurs when all your contingencies expire.

HML: Hard-money lender.

Holdback: Any time a lender holds back funds from a loan. These would be held in escrow and released based upon the agreement. Holdbacks could be for interest payments, future taxes or insurance, construction, unsatisfied liens or judgments, or satisfying a title requirement.

Junk (hidden) fees: Fees that are normally in addition to the expected fees, such as loan origination or title insurance.

Lien: This is a right to the property, and depending on the lien can give the lienholder the right to foreclose. Liens can show up on the property with or without the owner consent. Obviously when the owner takes out a loan there will be a lien, but an owner can also find a lien on their property for not paying contractors, taxes, HOA fees, child support, unpaid judgments, fines, or a number of other reasons. Properties generally cannot be refinanced or sold without satisfying liens, so they are an effective way to be sure debt gets paid.

Loan-to-cost (LTC): Loan-to-cost is a ratio used by lenders to determine the amount of a down payment. Some lenders include closing costs and interest in this ratio, and some do not, so you will see some variance. Most lenders have maximum LTC ratios that must be met to qualify for the loan making a down payment a requirement.

Loan-to-value (LTV): Loan-to-value is another ratio used by lenders to determine the amount of equity in a property. Most hard-money lenders care more about this ratio than the LTC ratio because they are focused on their position in the property in the event of a default. The most common LTV ratio is 70 percent.

Maximum allowable offer (MAO): Maximum allowable offer is the most a real estate investor should pay for a house. This is calculated using the MOA formula discussed in this book.

Mezzanine (Mezz): A form of subordinate financing used by experienced real estate investors and lenders. These loans can be secured by a junior position loan or by other assets, such as ownership in the company. In no event would a mezz lender be a senior lien on a property, so most hard-money lenders will not do them.

Mortgage: This is the lien on the property that secures a loan. Much like a deed of trust, it details what rights the lender has under certain circumstances and give the lender the right to force place insurance, secure the property, make repairs, and foreclose if there is a default. Mortgages are used in states that require a judicial foreclosure process which means the foreclosure goes through a court process before the house can be auctioned off to the public or repossessed by the lender.

Net operating income (NOI): Net operating income is the final income a property will produce before accounting for any loans. It recognizes the gross potential rent and then subtracts for vacancies and expenses. It is an extremely important number in calculating profits, returns, and values.

Personal financial statement (PFS): Personal financial statements are used by lenders to qualify borrowers. Experienced real estate investors keep an updated PFS to provide to lenders when requested. These statements include personal info, income, expenses, assets, and liabilities.

Proof of funds (POF): Proof of funds is proof that you have the money to close. If you offer all cash, the seller will most likely want to see you have the funds to close. If you are using hard money, you are not providing proof of funds, you would be providing a loan commitment. Letter. Although those two do get mixed up in this industry, true proof of funds shows that *you* have the money to close.

Points: These are fees. If they are lender points, each point represents one percent of the loan amount in a fee. One point is always equal to one percent.

Qualified mortgage (QM): In the wake of the 2008 credit crash, the Dodd Frank Act of 2010 was signed into law. This massive piece of legislation, also known as financial reform, is more than 2,300 pages and is intended to solve countless financial problems. A large part of Dodd Frank is focused on mortgage lending, and a piece of that defines Qualified Mortgages. QMs were defined to help standardize residential lending create fairness and transparency. Here are some of the guidelines for a loan to qualify as QM at the time of this writing.

- Terms of less than 30 years
- Lenders cannot charge points and fees exceeding three percent of the loan amount
- Debt-to-income ratios must be less than 43 percent
- Income must be fully documented
- No interest only or negative amortization loans
- No balloon payments (these loans must be fully amortized)

Most business lenders, including hard money and private money, are considered non-QM. For that reason, they do not fall under these restrictions.

Settlement sheet: This has the same meaning as a closing statement. This is the document that discloses how the title company is handling the funds. It details where the money for the transaction is coming from and where it is going.

Soft costs: These are the costs in a construction project that are not tangible. These include the permits, the diligence reports, the plans, the engineering, and other city or utility fees.

Take down: This is closing on a deal. Many investors think of looking for a deal as a hunt, and once you find the prey, you take it down. You might hear borrowers asking for hard-money or bridge financing for the take down. In that case, they only want the money for the acquisition and then they will have alternative financing in the background that will be used to refinance the "take down" loan or for other improvements.

Vacancy clause: A clause found in many insurance policies that will not allow a home to sit vacant. The clauses says that if a house sits vacant for too long, normally 30 days or more, the policy is void.

Wholesaler: A real estate investor who finds great deals that they sell to other real estate investors. Normally there is a small fee, known as the wholesale fee, paid to the wholesaler as their profit for locating the deal.

Appendix

Maximum Loan Worksheet

Rental analysis. Calculating the maximum loan amount for a property.

_____ Monthly rent

- _____ Vacancy ← | 5–10% |

- _____ Maintenance ← | 10–15% Single family
10–30% Multifamily |

- _____ Taxes & insurance

- _____ Other expenses (utilities, admin fees,

management fees)

= _____ NOI

- _____ Required cash flow

= _____ Max principal & interest

Max loan amount

Visit www.fundyourflip.com to get a free worksheet with amortization calculator.

MAO

_____ / _____ = _____

(Max loan)   (Lender required LTV)   (Maximum offer)

MAO: What to Offer?
(Max Loan Method)

Max loan: _____ * 70% = _____
                (ARV)

Closing costs: _____ * 2% + $3,000 = _____
                     (max loan)

Offer price:

_____ Max loan

- _____ Repairs

- _____ Closing costs

= _____ Max offer

(Profit Method)

List Price _____

_____ Sale price (ARV)

- _____ Profit

- _____ CC (purchase)

- _____ Repairs

- _____ Holding costs ←

- _____ Concessions

- _____ Realtor fees

- _____ CC (Sell)

		# of Months	
Interest payments	_____ x	___ =	_____
HOA	+ _____ x	___ =	_____
Insurance	+ _____ x	___ =	_____
Taxes	+ _____ x	___ =	_____
Utilities	+ _____ x	___ =	_____
Total	=	_____	

= _____ Max offer

Cash to Close Worksheet

Calculate Debits

Closing Costs: _____ * 3% + $2,000 = _____
                        (loan)

Monthly Payment: _____ * 12.9% / 12 months = _____
                            (loan)

Prepaid Items: _____ / 2 + $1,000 = _____
                        (monthly payment)

Total Debits: _____ + _____
                        (purchase price)   (Repairs)

+_____ + _____ = _____
        (Closing Costs)   (prepaid items)

Calculate Credits

Total Credits: _____ + _____ = _____
                        (loan)   (Earnest money)

Cash To Close

Cash To Close: _____ - _____ = [   ]
                        (Debits)   (Credits)

About the Author

Kevin Amolsch is a successful real estate investor and private-money lender. He formed Pine Financial Group, Inc. in 2008 after leaving a small mortgage company as the senior loan officer for residential lending. Kevin has a degree in finance, which he obtained after serving four years in the US Army. Starting out in banking, he worked in the lending department while working toward his degree. From there he started his first real estate investment company, which is still active today.

After college, Kevin spent two years working with Wall Street as a mortgage bond analyst before leaving to work as a loan officer with real estate investors full time. He and his companies have closed on over 2,500 transactions with a combined value of more than $1 billion as a buyer, seller, or private-money lender. He has spent more than 20 years as a real estate investor and 16 years in real estate lending. He is the author of the best-selling book *The 45-Day Investor* and a frequent speaker. He has been quoted in the *Las Vegas Review Journal*, the *Denver Post*, the *Denver Business Journal*, *Forbes*, and *Yahoo! Real Estate*.

When he is not helping his team or clients make more money in real estate, he is spending time with his family or can be found on a trail. He loves snowboarding, hiking, mountain biking, and all that his home state of Colorado has to offer.

Made in United States
Troutdale, OR
11/19/2023

14721060R00086